PRESIDENT
BLING BLING

MONSTERS

Other books by the author:

Gerald Scarfe's People

Indecent Exposure

Expletive Deleted: The Life and Times of Richard Nixon

Gerald Scarfe

Father Kissmas and Mother Claus

Scarfeland – A Lost World of Fabulous Beasts & Monsters

Scarfe by Scarfe

Scarfe's Seven Deadly Sins

Scarfe: Line of Attack

Scarfe on Stage

Scarfeface

Hades – The Truth at Last

Heroes & Villains: Scarfe at the National Portrait Gallery

Drawing Blood – Forty-five Years of Scarfe Uncensored

Gerald Scarfe

MONSTERS

How George Bush Saved the World and Other Tall Stories

Little, Brown

LITTLE, BROWN

First published in Great Britain in 2008 by Little, Brown

A CIP catalogue record for this book is available from the British Library.

ISBN 978-1-4087-0085-3

Typeset in Garamond 3

Printed and bound in China

Design: Sian Rance, D.R. ink

Little, Brown
An imprint of
Little, Brown Book Group
100 Victoria Embankment
London EC4Y 0DY

An Hachette Livre UK Company
www.hachettelivre.co.uk

www.littlebrown.co.uk

With special thanks to Julie Davies for her patient dedication in curating and scanning this book and for assembling the endpapers

Thanks also to:
Caroline Stacey
Dan Balado-Lopez
Emil Dacanay
Nick Ross
Richard Beswick
Sheila Rance
Sian Rance
Theo Dacanay
Vivien Redman

And, as always, with thanks to my wife Jane

To my family

CONTENTS

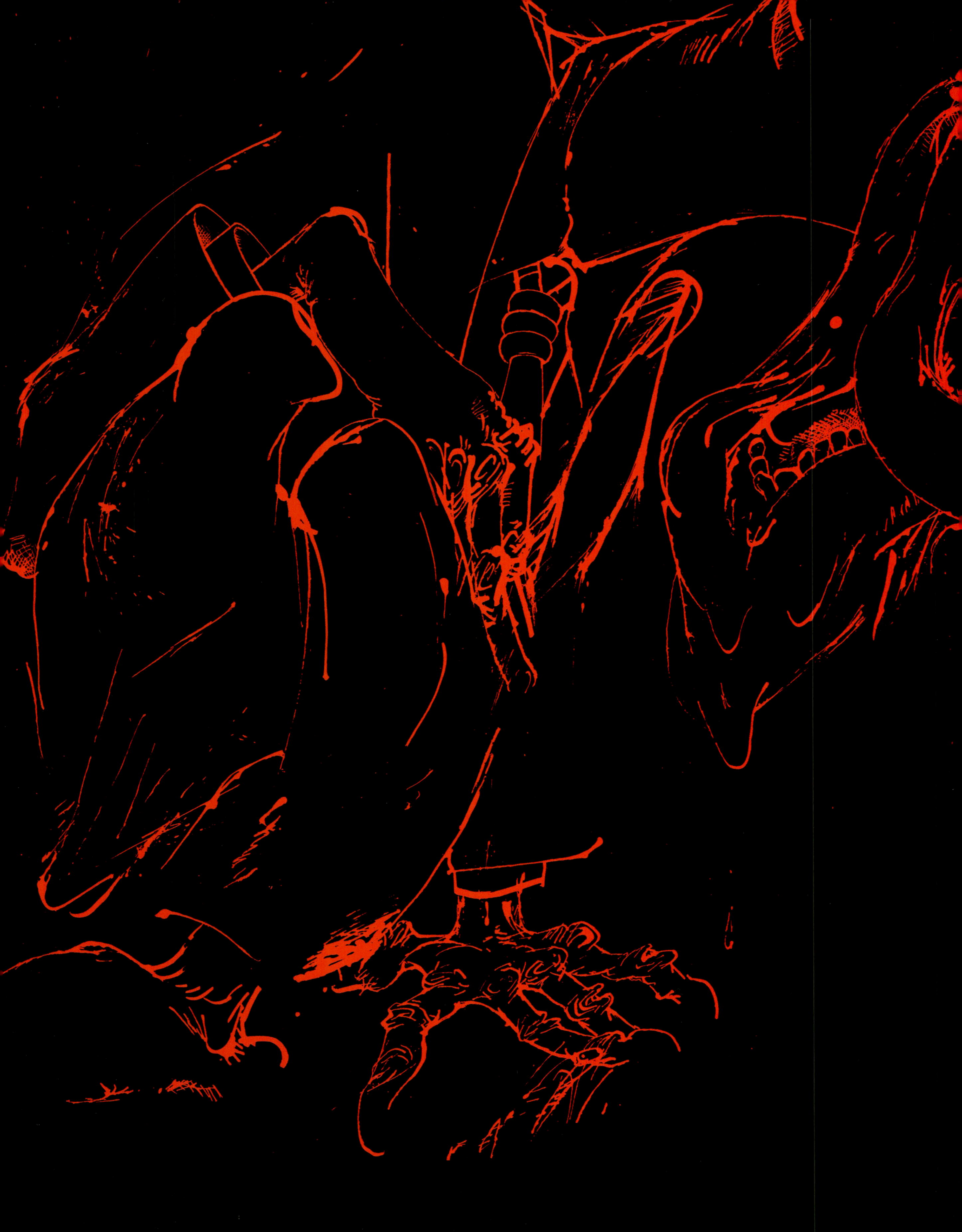

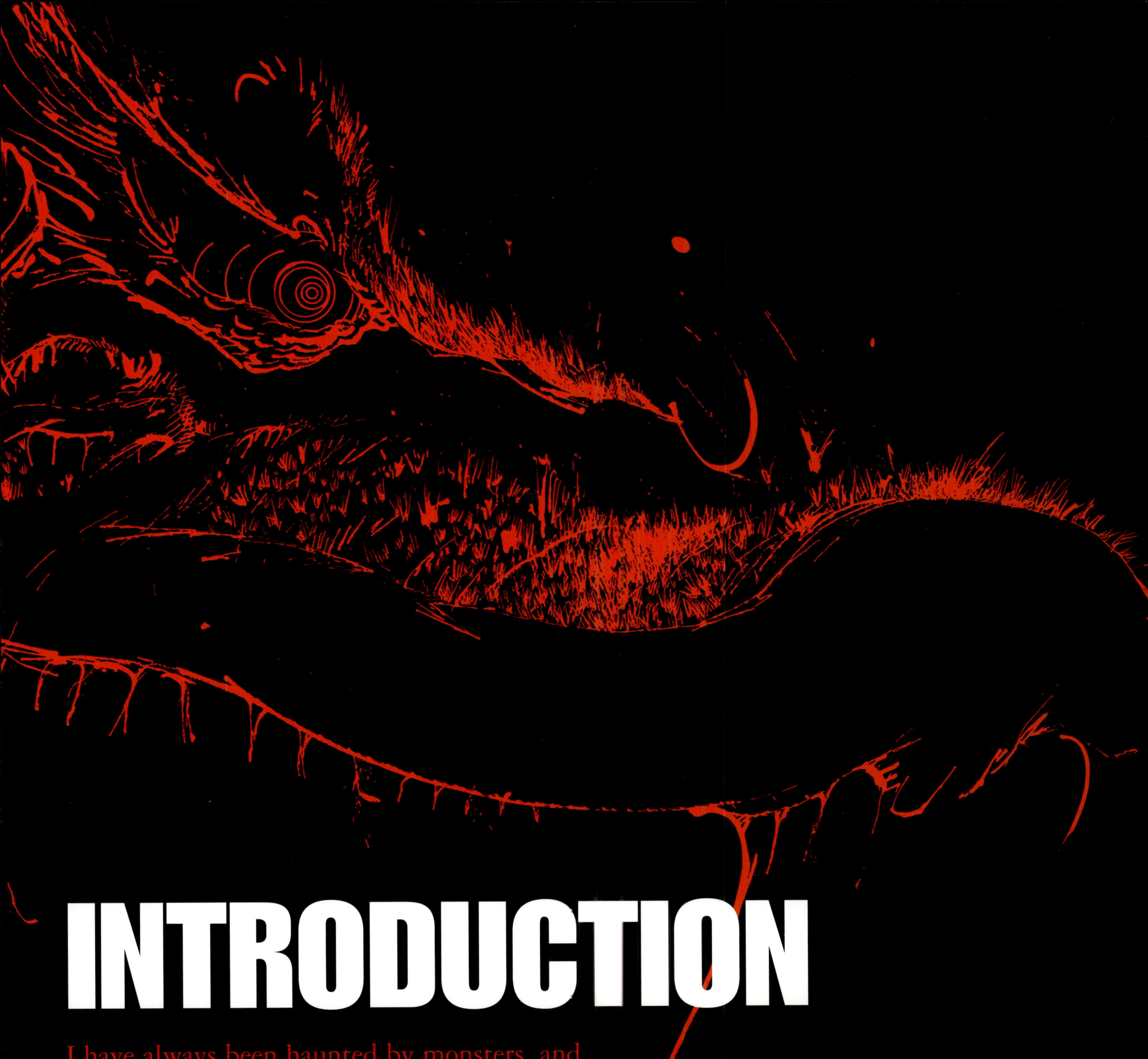

INTRODUCTION

I have always been haunted by monsters, and now the monsters of my childhood nightmares seem to rule the world. Fifty years of monstrous presidents, prime ministers, dictators, tyrants and politicians stalk these pages: some merely monstrously arrogant, devious and inept; others corrupt, wicked and murderous.

I think they enjoy it . . .

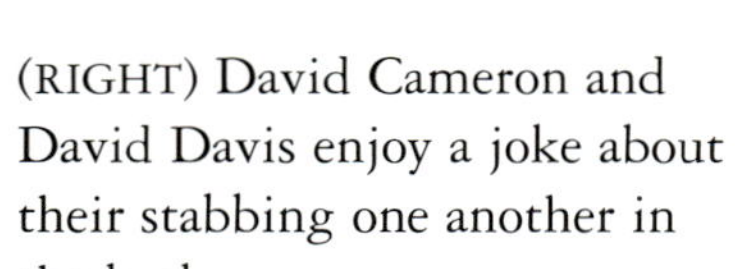

(RIGHT) David Cameron and David Davis enjoy a joke about their stabbing one another in the back.

(BELOW) The shit politician.

What a ghastly, motley crew they are – so many making the same old mistakes, filching and trousering tax payers' cash, screwing their secretaries and getting caught with their pants around their ankles, pie-eyed with booze: clowns drunk with their own power and, even worse, the war-mongers, torturers and murderers. Power is what they want, and to get it they snarl and fight and bite. They stab one another in the back and they lie and lie. They have no shame – the unkept promises, the terrible, terrible mistakes that end in thousands of deaths.

In this book you can find the lying burglar who was a president; the braggart who boasted he had a bigger penis than Mao; the poodle who took us to war on a lie; the monster who kept his opponents' heads in his fridge; and the president who unleashed a swathe of atrocities and persecution across the world on a misconception.

It's still the same old story – a fight for love and glory. Although love is often lust and glory is often gory. However, there's nothing like a bit of sex and violence to make a story nip along, or a drawing a bit more exciting.

I believe politicians would rather be drawn as a lump of snot on a pig's nose than be ignored.

(LEFT) Blair's fantasy

(BELOW) Blair's final hours

My only respite is to pin these characters to the paper with a steely nib; but you can hit a politician as hard as you like and he bounces back. You try it – it's true. I think they enjoy it – it's all grist to their mill. Such is their desire for attention I believe politicians would rather be drawn as a lump of snot on a pig's nose than be ignored. When cartooned, however viciously, it means they have arrived, that they are recognised, even if that recognition is for the most dreadful deeds. I doubt that a cartoon changes their course at all – some say it's an honour: none say, 'Oh – I see the error of my ways! I shall dedicate myself to charity in future . . . '

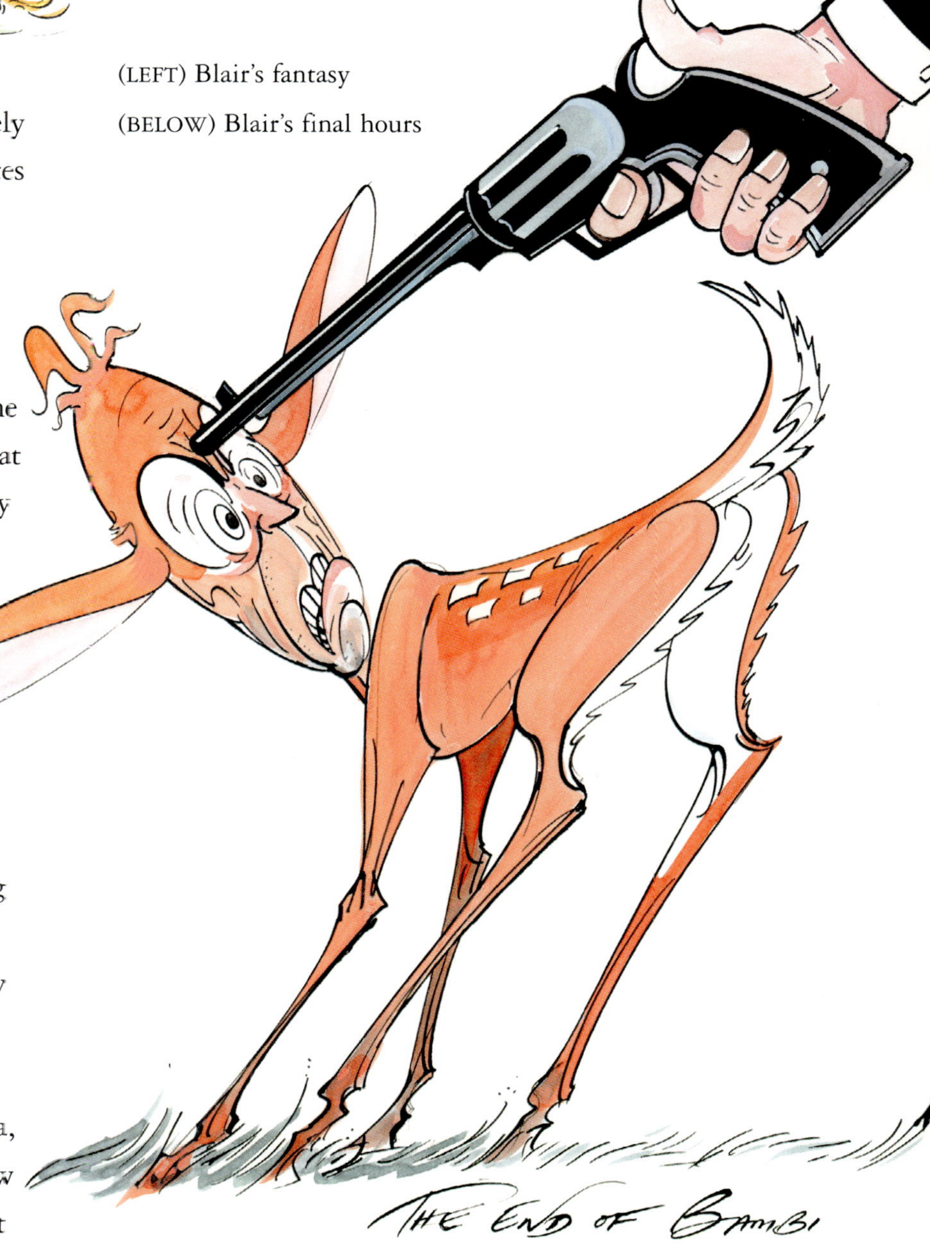

Some monsters are walking caricatures, others seem to have no features of any interest at all. In a way, these are the more interesting, because they are harder nuts to crack. Ultimately everybody is caricaturable, and whatever arrangement a cartoonist arrives at with his readers he can lead them to know that, for instance, a grinning poodle represents Tony Blair. I remember, when Margaret Thatcher was first elected leader of the Conservative Party very little was known about her outside political circles. Who was she? But once she became prime minister, because of her position of power, events began to influence her public persona, and I could draw her as an axe, a battleship, a bitch, a mad cow or even an old bag, still leaving, I hope, the reader in no doubt as to who it was.

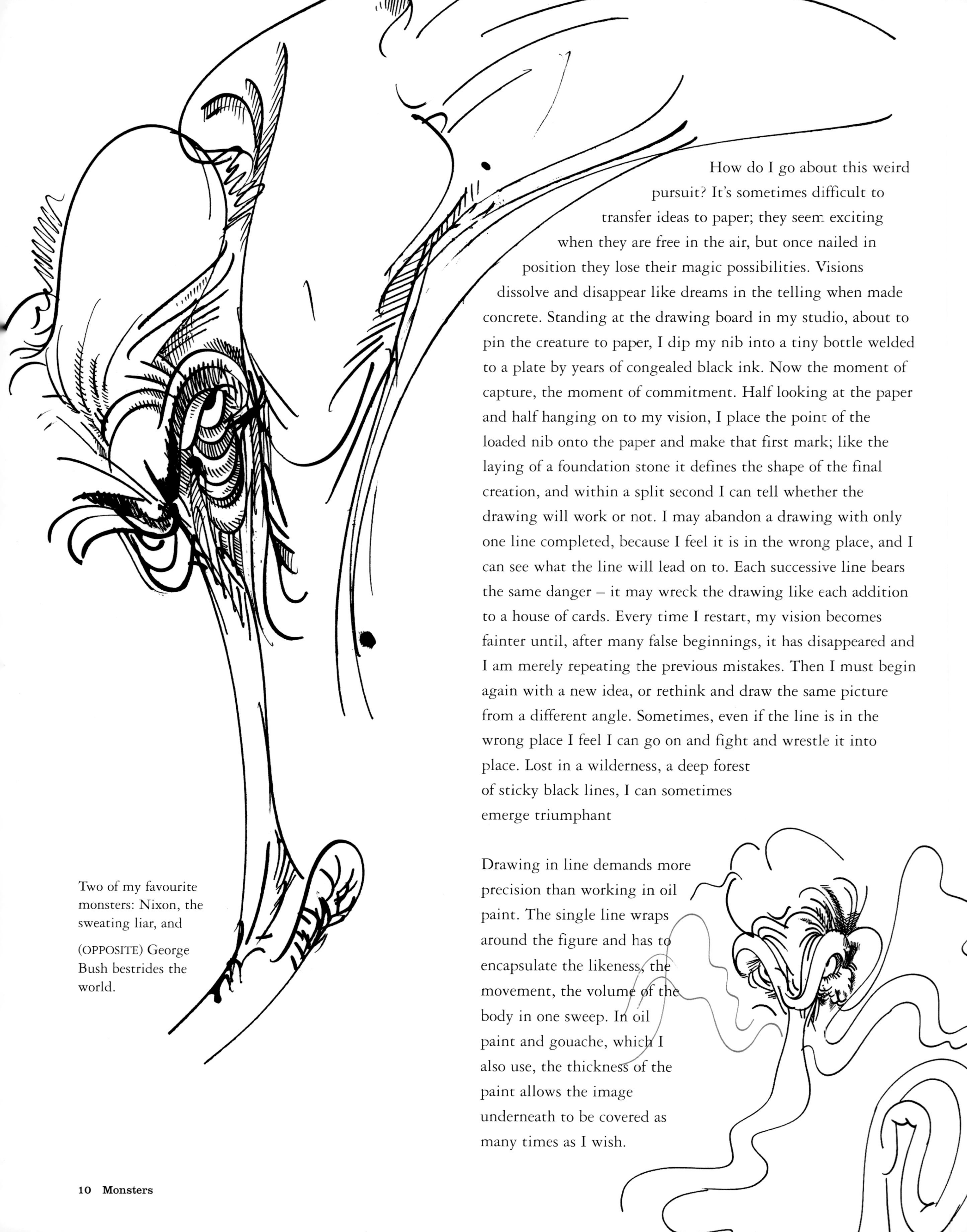

How do I go about this weird pursuit? It's sometimes difficult to transfer ideas to paper; they seem exciting when they are free in the air, but once nailed in position they lose their magic possibilities. Visions dissolve and disappear like dreams in the telling when made concrete. Standing at the drawing board in my studio, about to pin the creature to paper, I dip my nib into a tiny bottle welded to a plate by years of congealed black ink. Now the moment of capture, the moment of commitment. Half looking at the paper and half hanging on to my vision, I place the point of the loaded nib onto the paper and make that first mark; like the laying of a foundation stone it defines the shape of the final creation, and within a split second I can tell whether the drawing will work or not. I may abandon a drawing with only one line completed, because I feel it is in the wrong place, and I can see what the line will lead on to. Each successive line bears the same danger – it may wreck the drawing like each addition to a house of cards. Every time I restart, my vision becomes fainter until, after many false beginnings, it has disappeared and I am merely repeating the previous mistakes. Then I must begin again with a new idea, or rethink and draw the same picture from a different angle. Sometimes, even if the line is in the wrong place I feel I can go on and fight and wrestle it into place. Lost in a wilderness, a deep forest of sticky black lines, I can sometimes emerge triumphant

Drawing in line demands more precision than working in oil paint. The single line wraps around the figure and has to encapsulate the likeness, the movement, the volume of the body in one sweep. In oil paint and gouache, which I also use, the thickness of the paint allows the image underneath to be covered as many times as I wish.

Two of my favourite monsters: Nixon, the sweating liar, and (OPPOSITE) George Bush bestrides the world.

While drawing a character I feel as though I am acting him – just as an impersonator picks up the movements and characteristics of that person.

While drawing a character I feel as though I am acting him – just as an impersonator picks up the movements and characteristics of that person, I can hear his voice and I can see him move, and I impersonate the 3D character in ink and paint on to two-dimensional paper.

There is an overall image that all people transmit and it is possible to convince the onlooker, even without the correct proportions or indeed features, that it is that person. At other times when I am not clearly seeing the total image, I can draw the correct nose, mouth, eyes, ears, etc, but when they are assembled on the paper they do not add up to a likeness.

Speed of delivery is essential when working for a newspaper like the *Sunday Times*. The drawings must be topical and easy to read, and the ideas must come across immediately and clearly. It all has to be squeezed out before the dreaded deadline, which, when it descends, cuts off any further work: I may have a better idea, or want to add more detail, but – tough! The guillotine has fallen.

I get a particular satisfaction from drawing politicians as animals. I know this is insulting to animals but it can be boring drawing the same people time after time. I saw Harold Wilson as a crafty old toad, puffing and swelling with self-congratulatory pleasure. Jim Callaghan was a sly pig, snuffling and snouting for truffles in the political sty. Margaret Thatcher was a pterodactyl, with a razor-sharp beak, wheeling on leathery wings through a yellow prehistoric sky, swooping low on her victims with blood-red talons. Ian Smith was the almost extinct white rhinoceros. Enoch Powell the hound of the Baskervilles, baying for immigrants' blood. Dr David Owen, once the strutting peacock, then the dodo. Richard Nixon was the rogue Republican elephant, a sad, sagging leather sack hung on whitened bones, bleached in the heat of the Watergate sun.

I have always been haunted by monsters, and now the monsters of my childhood nightmares seem to rule the world.

(TOP) The author in his studio.

(RIGHT) Sketch for the New Roman

He had gone to die in the elephants' graveyard. Blair, of course, the bouncy deluded poodle, permed and coiffed, eager to please his master, waiting for a special treat from that nice Mr Bush. I see Bush as a mad ape, swinging from thought to thought and then colliding with reality. How the hell did he get there?

Now it's Brown, the sulky, morose black bear, stinking and grumbling in his corner.

The big and little tin-pot generals come and go; people continue to be slaughtered and starved and used as cannon fodder. It is the misuse of power, from the smallest, crookedest local councillor to the biggest, bloodiest Stalin, that fires my political drawings.

Gerald Scarfe
August 2008

RAQ
HERCULES
BY APPOINTMENT

Monstrous Environment

Behold, the environment created and inhabited by Monsters.

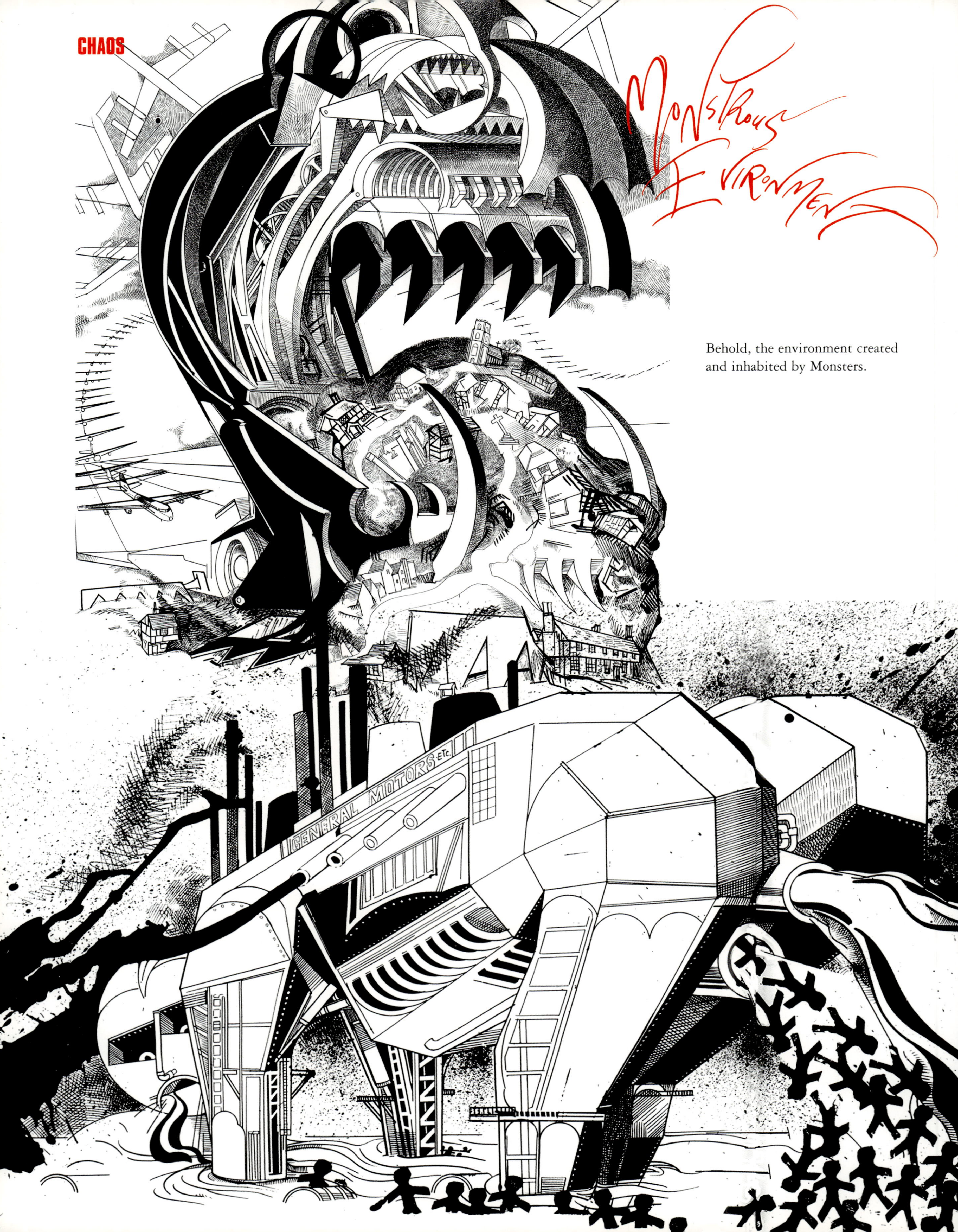

SKY CATTLE
AIR CHAOS
NERVE GAS
GAS
GAS
Arrabs
ICES £20
MARKS & SPENDSOME
←SHOPLIFTING
ROYALTY £1 A GAPE
RIP OFF

Christine Keeler as *The Naked Maya* by Goya. Macmillan seated on a chair in a pose echoing the famous photograph. (*Private Eye*)

I cut my teeth on Harold Macmillan. He and the Profumo affair were a gift.

'In 1963 *Private Eye* published a simple cartoon by Gerald Scarfe that marked the beginning of an era. It depicted the prime minister, Harold Macmillan, corpulent and simpering, perched on an Arne Jacobson chair: what was extraordinary about it was that Macmillan was naked. Parodying the iconic photograph of Christine Keeler, similarly perched, its deft equation of the great and the bad – as the Profumo scandle rumbled on – was utterly liberating. If any one cartoon marked the rejuvenation of insult and aggression in graphic satire, Scarfe's was it, since no major figure of state had been ridiculed in his nakedness since the 1790s. Cartooning of this audacity opened the way to others and helped focus a public scepticism about the great and not so good that had long lacked a language.'

VIC GATRELL, FELLOW OF CAIUS COLLEGE, CAMBRIDGE.

HAROLD MACMILLAN

PRIME MINISTER 1957–1963

'. . . you've never had it so good'

Macmillan sits dejectedly in front of the Profumo orgy at Cliveden.

MACMILLAN **MAC THE KNIFE**

Echoing the 'Night of the Long Knives' of both Hitler (1934) and Macmillan (1962), leadership contenders circle towards the end of 1963 as Macmillan, sunk by scandal and ill health, resigns. (From bottom left, clockwise) Lord Boothby, allegedly the lover of Dorothy Macmillan, Harold's wife; Tory minister Ernest Marples – head only; Duncan Sandys, thought to be the 'headless man' in the compromising photographs at the 1963 divorce trial of Margaret, Duchess of Argyll ('headless' because the Polaroid showed only a torso being pleasured by the duchess; in the fullness of time it turned out to be Douglas Fairbanks, Jr.); Rab Butler; Lord Hailsham; Lord Home; Ted Heath; Macmillan (in the wheelchair); and the Chancellor, Reginald Maudling. The central figures are Tory minister Iain Macleod (top) and Henry Brooke, Home Secretary (bottom).

Macmillan as the patrician gentleman on the grouse moors (BELOW); then (RIGHT) as an older man in 1976, warning Britain, in stark contrast to his famous quote from 1957, that they have had it. Iain Macleod (seated) was briefly Chancellor of the Exchequer in the Heath government (1970–4).

General de Gaulle, as proprietorial towards the gall bladder he had removed as he was towards Europe; and (OPPOSITE) in the pose of the Marquis de Sade, refusing Britain entry into the Common Market for a second time, in 1967.

De Gaulle
Dits
Non!
Maquis De Gaulle

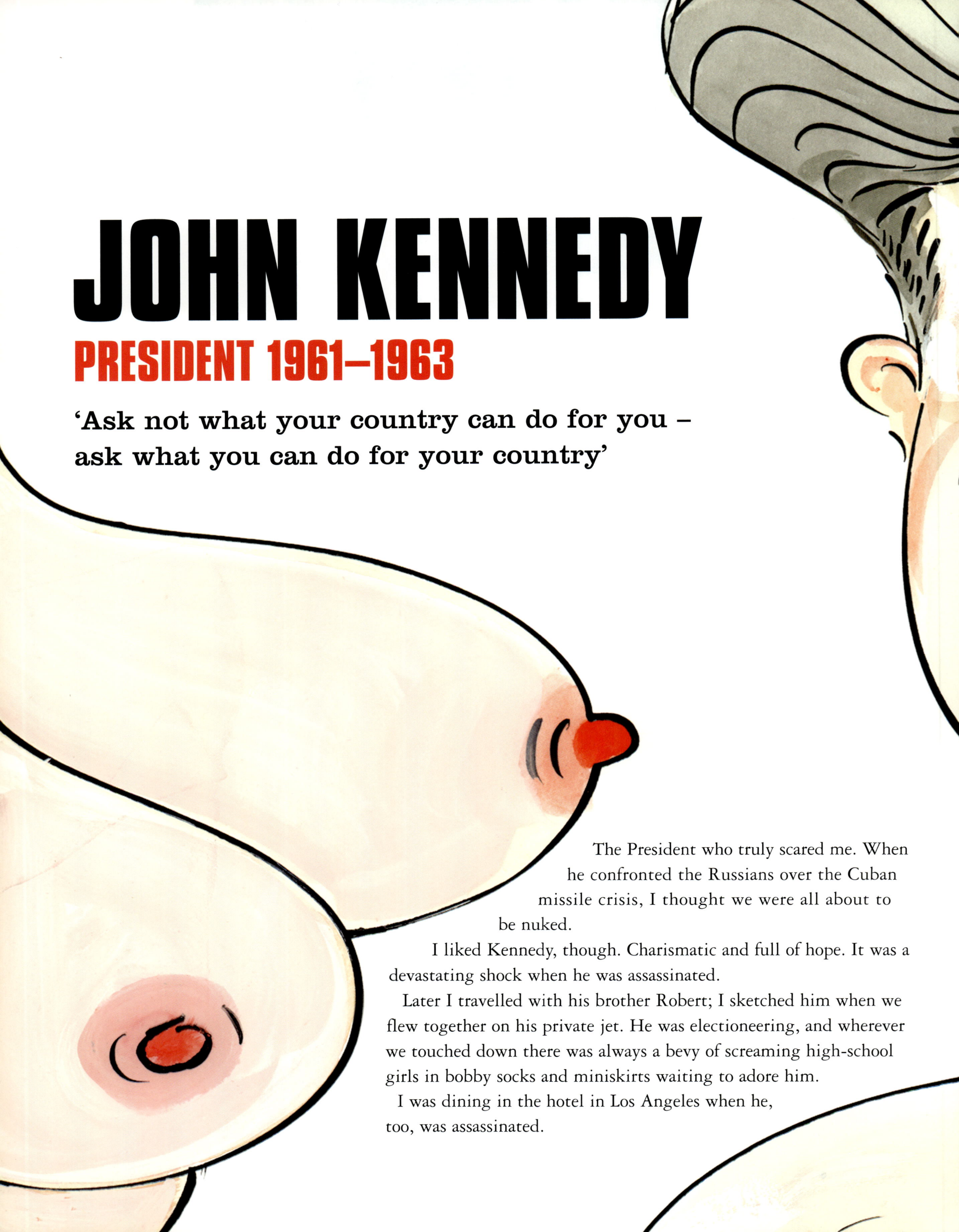

JOHN KENNEDY

PRESIDENT 1961–1963

'Ask not what your country can do for you – ask what you can do for your country'

The President who truly scared me. When he confronted the Russians over the Cuban missile crisis, I thought we were all about to be nuked.

I liked Kennedy, though. Charismatic and full of hope. It was a devastating shock when he was assassinated.

Later I travelled with his brother Robert; I sketched him when we flew together on his private jet. He was electioneering, and wherever we touched down there was always a bevy of screaming high-school girls in bobby socks and miniskirts waiting to adore him.

I was dining in the hotel in Los Angeles when he, too, was assassinated.

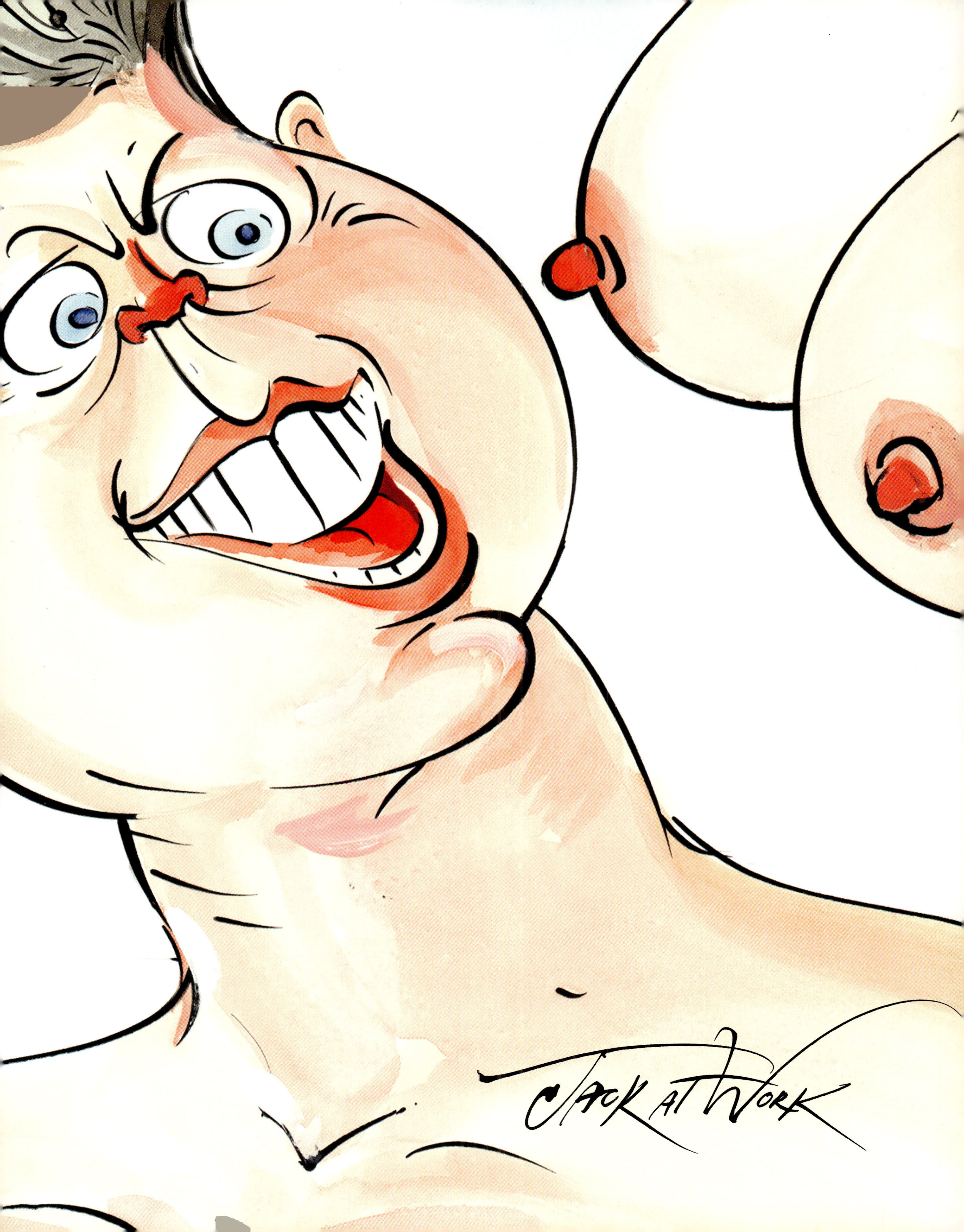
JACK AT WORK

Gorillas in the Streets

Assassination

(LEFT) Gorillas in the streets. This was my feeling about the violence in New York on my first visit in 1964.

(ABOVE) The Kennedy brothers. Jack plays roulette with the world during the Cuban missile crisis in 1962; Ted, who like all his brothers had a reputation for womanising (the big scandal at the time concerned the death of Mary Jo Kopechne in the back seat of Ted's car, which had plunged into a river off a narrow bridge on the East Coast island of Chappaquiddick); and Robert, the third and youngest brother, an attractive, charismatic character who was, like his brother, assassinated, in 1968.

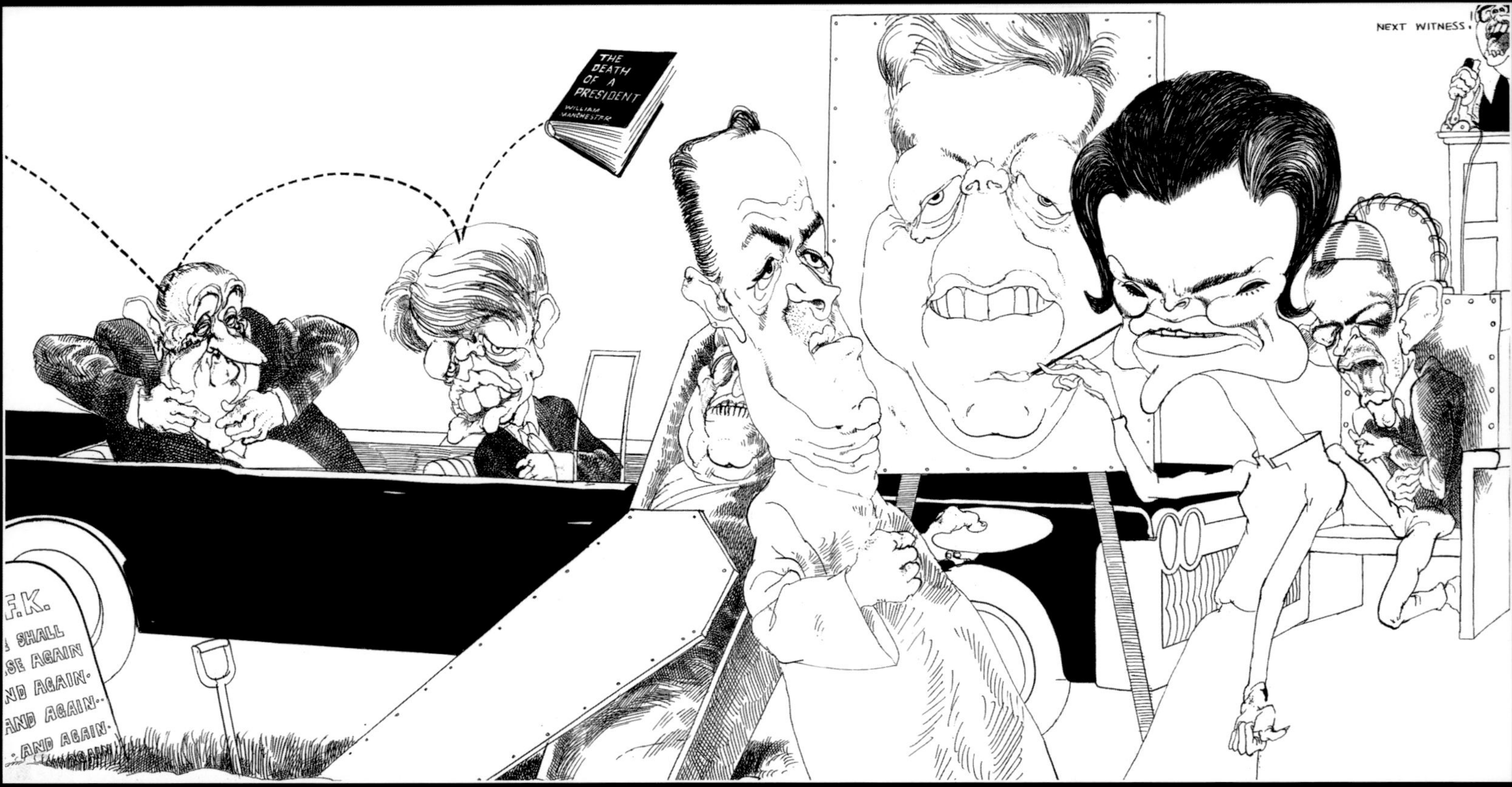

(ABOVE) Lyndon Johnson and Robert Kennedy being hit on the head by William Manchester's *The Death of a President* while the body of Jack lies in a coffin beside the limo. Manchester himself and Jacqueline Kennedy paint the picture of Jack. On the right is Lee Harvey Oswald, controversially collared for the shooting of JFK, who would almost certainly have fried had Jack Ruby not got to him first.

(LEFT) My feelings about America at the time. In the centre, the burning of an African American watched by a Ku Klux Klan member. To the left, a riot policeman and his vicious dog attacking an African American child. On the right, Kennedy about to press the button for nuclear war. Such were the fears we had then about a nuclear accident . . .

(OPPOSITE) Ted Kennedy, the remaining brother from the hydra-like Kennedy clan, runs with the ball while his two brothers lie dead on the pitch behind him.

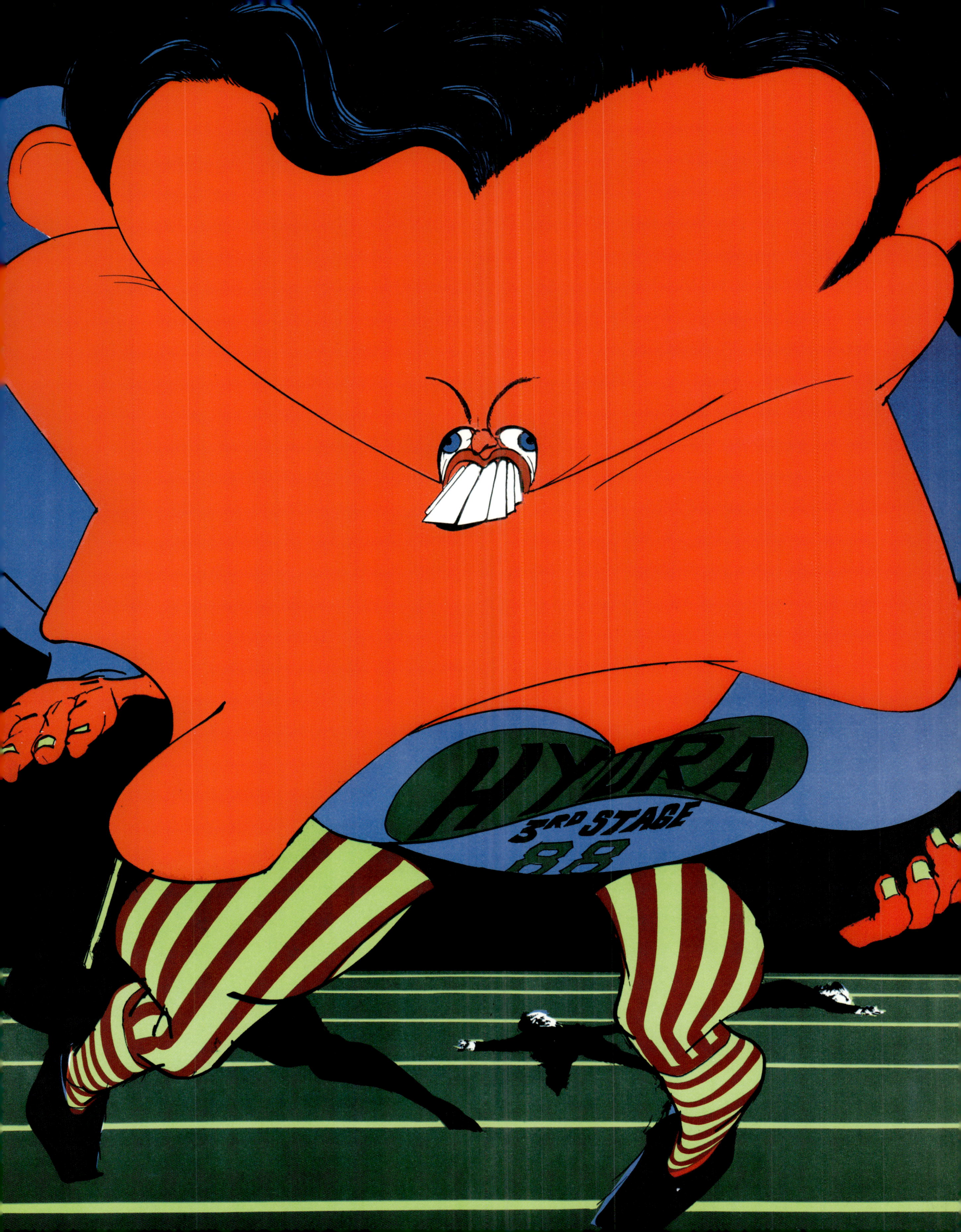
HYDRA
3RD STAGE
88

(BELOW) Leonid Brezhnev and Prime Minister Alexei Kosygin (extreme right) resuscitated the spirit of Stalin in 1968–9 when Warsaw Pact forces occupied Czechoslovakia and the country's reforming First Secretary Alexander Dubček (bottom) was pressurised to stand down.

(OPPOSITE) Dubček, in a scene reminiscent of Eisenstein's film *Battleship Potemkin*; Hungary lies at the foot of the steps, already crushed. It was felt at the time that the fate of Eastern Europe was as much of a good cause as the situation in Vietnam.

DON'T I MAKE A FASHIONABLE CAUSE?
FAIR DEAL FOR STUDENTS
HANDS OFF VIET NAM
HO! HO! HO CHI MINH!
HUNGARY

'There are two problems in my life: the political ones are insoluble and the economic ones are incomprehensible'

LORD HOME

PRIME MINISTER 1963–1964

Another gift to draw. Willowy, faded and inadequate, he renounced his title in order to be Prime Minister, but remained the out-of-touch aristocrat. Head like a skull, with a little tongue that licked in and out like a lizard's, when he talked. Strangled voice, stiff upper lip – literally: it didn't move as he spoke, like a ventriloquist's dummy.

I travelled to Kinross with the *Private Eye* gang, when William Rushton stood against Home in the 1963 by-election. Rushton used one of my skull-like drawings as his campaign poster.

Home didn't last long.

HOME **DUMMY**

(LEFT) Lord Hailsham, aka Quintin Hogg – thought to be mad at the time.

(BELOW) Alec Douglas-Home as a ventriloquist's dummy on the knee of his Chancellor of the Exchequer, Reginald Maudling.

(OPPOSITE) Alec Douglas-Home 'prosecutes' Henry Brooke, his Home Secretary, who had made a number of deranged decisions.

IT'S ALL RIGHT-
HE WAS MENTALLY ILL
AT THE TIME

'Being president is like being a jackass in a hailstorm. There's nothing to do but stand there and take it'

Johnson was the old grafter, one of the good old boys.

I travelled with LBJ through Ohio down to Cape Canaveral, sketching him at every stop in the different towns. He always gave the same speech, but his voice became more and more deeply Southern the further south he went.

I remember the story of him coming in to greet awaiting journalists with 'Sorry I'm late, boys, but I've just been giving Lady Bird [his wife] one.' On another occasion he reportedly produced his appendage for the assembled journalists and said, 'Tell me now, boys, has Mao got one as big as this?'

LYNDON B. JOHNSON

US PRESIDENT 1963–1969

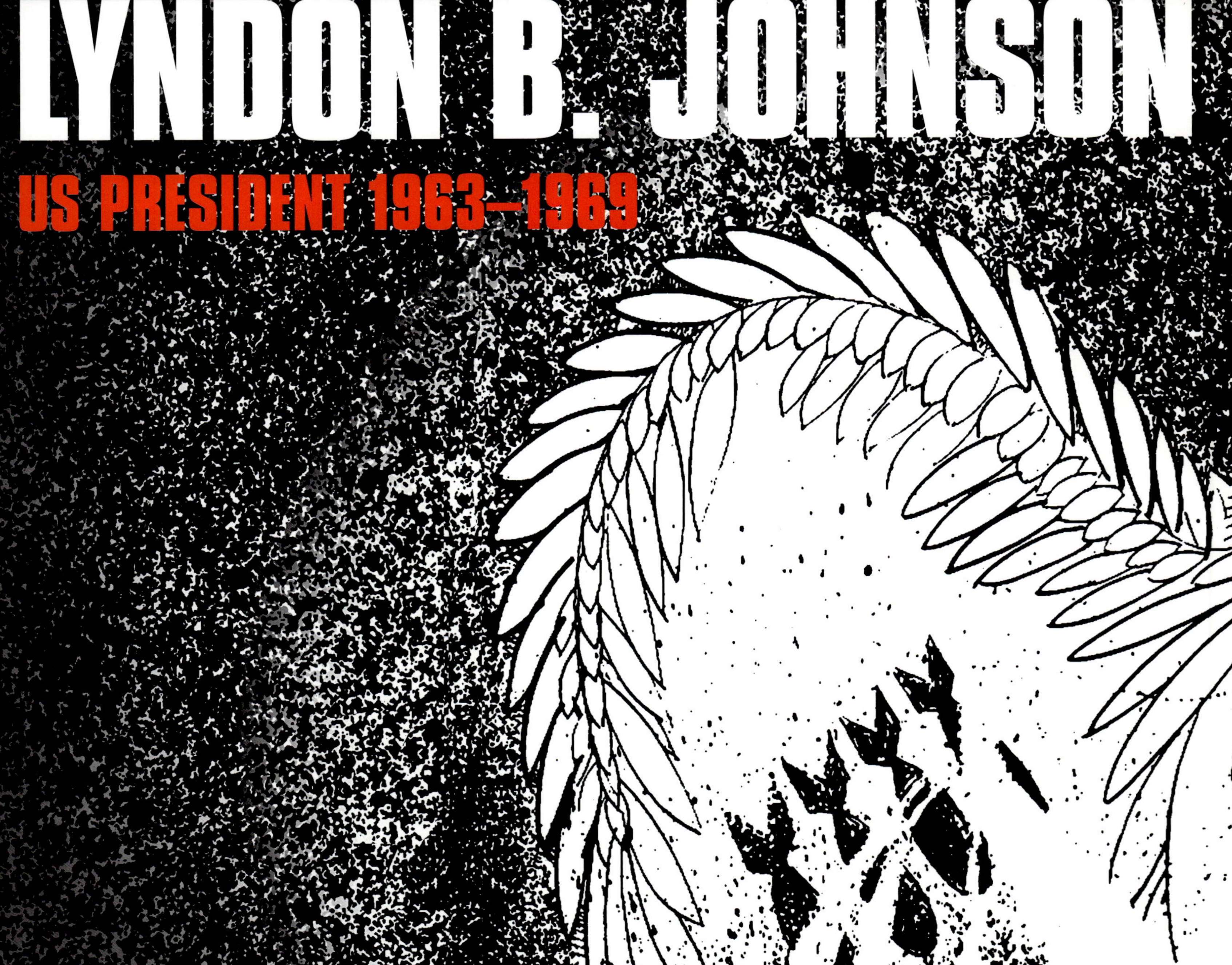

JOHNSON **HAWKS VIETNAM STRATEGY**

(BELOW) Lyndon Johnson and Viet Cong leader Ho Chi Minh tear apart the country of Vietnam, symbolised by a Vietnamese woman.

(MAIN PICTURE) Ho Chi Minh and LBJ, seated on the bodies of beautiful women (symbolising the beauty of North and South Vietnam), fire at each other. A hawk whispers in LBJ's ear. LBJ then descends like Moses from the mountain carrying the tablets of commandments. To the right we see him pointing the way to the American dream while his puppet premier in South Vietnam faces his countrymen.

JOHNSON INCONTINENCE
Coca-Cola
THOU SHALT NOT
UNGRATEFUL FOR
U.S. AID.
THOU SHALT NOT
KILL EXCEPT CHARLIE
THOU SHALT NOT
STEAL P.X. GOODS
THOU SHALT NO
INTERFERE WITH
THY ESCALATING
PACIFICATION
INDOCTRINATION
OR THY HIGHLY-
MOTIVATED RE-
CONSOLIDATED
RESETTLEMENT
PROGRAMME.
OU SHALT
VE NO OTHER
GOD.
P.T.O.

JOHNSON **OUT, OUT, DAMNED SPOT**

LBJ and his wife, Lady Bird Johnson, as Macbeth and Lady Macbeth.

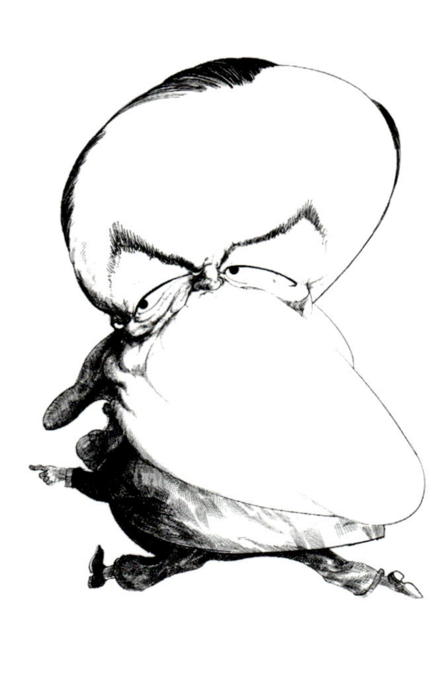

(FROM TOP LEFT, CLOCKWISE) George Wallace, Governor of Alabama; vice-president Hubert Humphrey being carried on LBJ's back; LBJ recalling General Westmoreland (the hawk) from Vietnam in an attempt to extricate himself from the mess of Vietnam as the 1968 election approaches; LBJ in the pose of Abraham Lincoln, a hawk whispering in his ear; hard-right Republican Senator Barry Goldwater, who ran against Johnson in the 1964 election; Wallace, carrying the flaming cross of the Ku Klux Klan (symbolising his racism), riding on the back of a general as he urges a hardline policy of bombing in Vietnam; and LBJ carrying the woes of office around his neck like Jacob Marley.

Wilson, having finally won out in the double election year of 1974, takes off like an inflated balloon towards his first crisis.

‘A week is a long time in politics’

HAROLD WILSON

PRIME MINISTER 1964–70 AND 1974–76

A little weasel of a man from Yorkshire. Round head, with a flat face drawn upon it; pouchy eyes, button nose and rodent’s mouth, full of rotting teeth. Insincere in his sincerity. Often seen in public smoking a pipe, playing the working man, although he actually smoked a cigar.

Not bad to draw, but his head was a circle. Impossible to caricature a circle: you can’t distort it without losing its essential shape.

I travelled as a correspondent with Wilson on a visit to somewhere or other. ‘What’s he bothered to come for?’ I was told he said about me. Shifty – eh, but they’re all shifty.

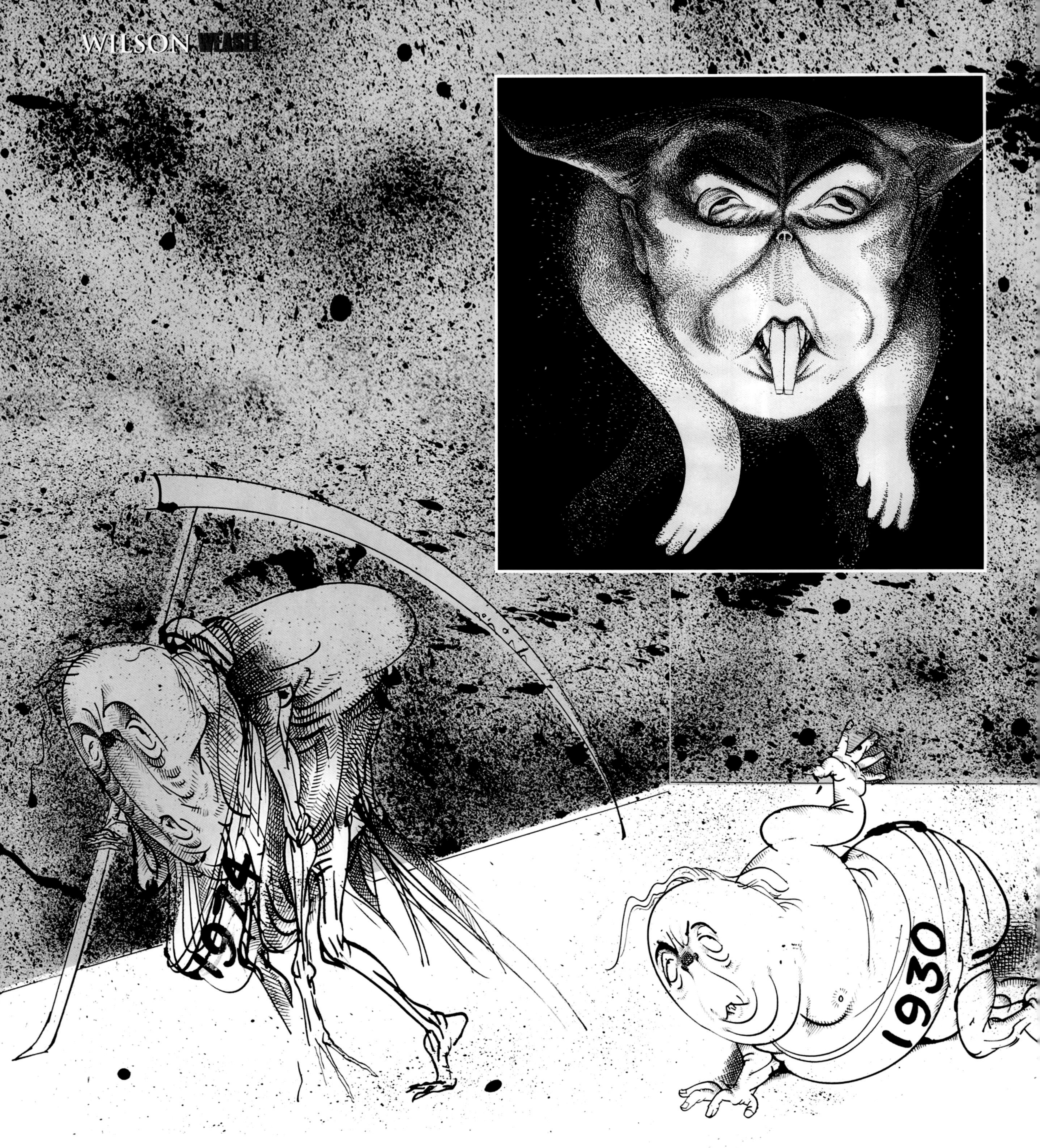
1974
1930

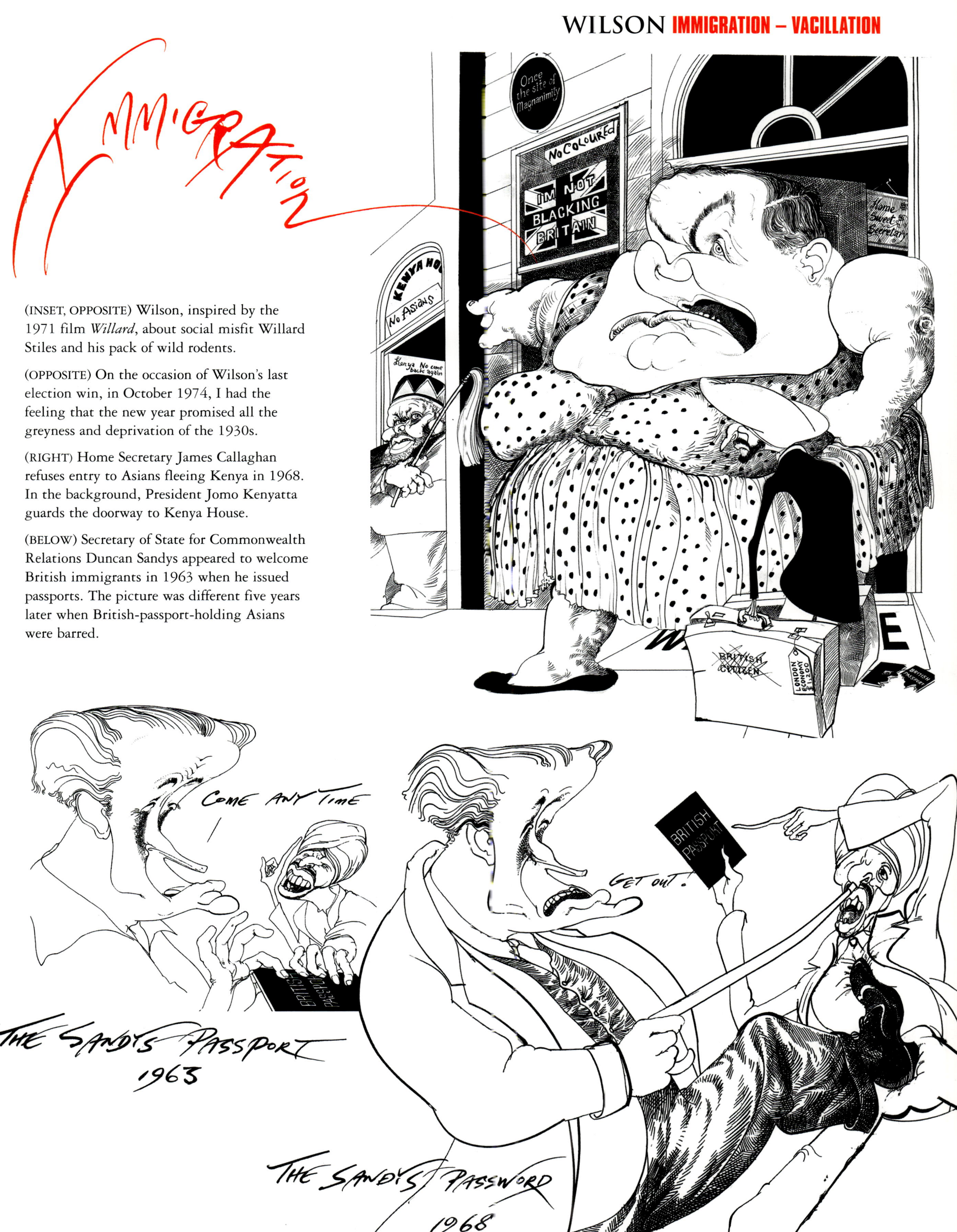

(INSET, OPPOSITE) Wilson, inspired by the 1971 film *Willard*, about social misfit Willard Stiles and his pack of wild rodents.

(OPPOSITE) On the occasion of Wilson's last election win, in October 1974, I had the feeling that the new year promised all the greyness and deprivation of the 1930s.

(RIGHT) Home Secretary James Callaghan refuses entry to Asians fleeing Kenya in 1968. In the background, President Jomo Kenyatta guards the doorway to Kenya House.

(BELOW) Secretary of State for Commonwealth Relations Duncan Sandys appeared to welcome British immigrants in 1963 when he issued passports. The picture was different five years later when British-passport-holding Asians were barred.

PIGS
IN
SHIT

(OPPOSITE) On top of the pile is Wilson; next to him are Liberal leader Jo Grimond and Alec Douglas-Home, sitting on the head of Rab Butler. Cabinet minister George Brown suckles Wilson, and both of them tread on the back of Lord Hailsham; Brown also sits on the head of former Tory Chancellor Selwyn Lloyd. Reginald Maudling (bottom right) swamps an almost drowning Henry Brooke.

Wilson in hock to the banks during the balance of payments crisis that badly affected his government's plans in the late sixties – represented here by a gaggle of lustful Swiss financiers.

George Brown, the highly colourful deputy prime minister who was eventually towed off to the House of Lords.

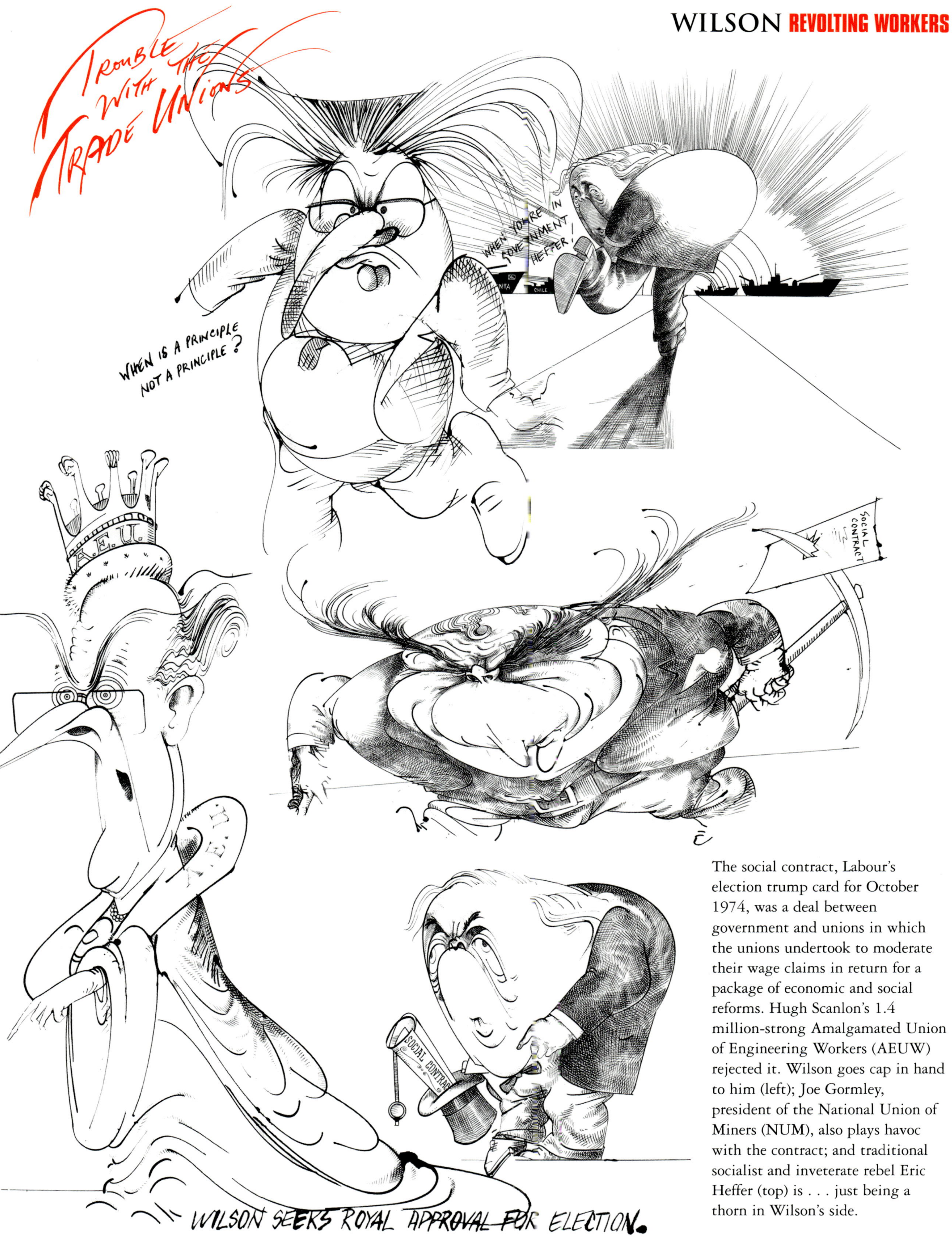

The social contract, Labour's election trump card for October 1974, was a deal between government and unions in which the unions undertook to moderate their wage claims in return for a package of economic and social reforms. Hugh Scanlon's 1.4 million-strong Amalgamated Union of Engineering Workers (AEUW) rejected it. Wilson goes cap in hand to him (left); Joe Gormley, president of the National Union of Miners (NUM), also plays havoc with the contract; and traditional socialist and inveterate rebel Eric Heffer (top) is . . . just being a thorn in Wilson's side.

PSSST!! THIS ELECTION IS ALL FOR NOTHING!
PAY BIRD
NO IT'S NOT— IT'S ALL FOR ME!
CON
PHASE I
PHASE II
PHASE III
AUTOMATIC
PAY LEAGUE TABLE
WAGES
Average Wage 100%
Mine Worker – 90%
Speculator 100,000%
CHAOS
AH! I SEE! THE CASH WAS IN THE TABLE NOT ON IT

Election day looms in February 1974 for (left to right) Gormley, the 'Pay Bird' Scanlon, Edward Heath, Alec Douglas-Home, Anthony Barber (Chancellor), Enoch Powell, Jim Callaghan (pushing the pram), Denis Healey, Roy Jenkins, Tony Benn, Harold Wilson (playing some old tunes) and Liberal leader Jeremy Thorpe.

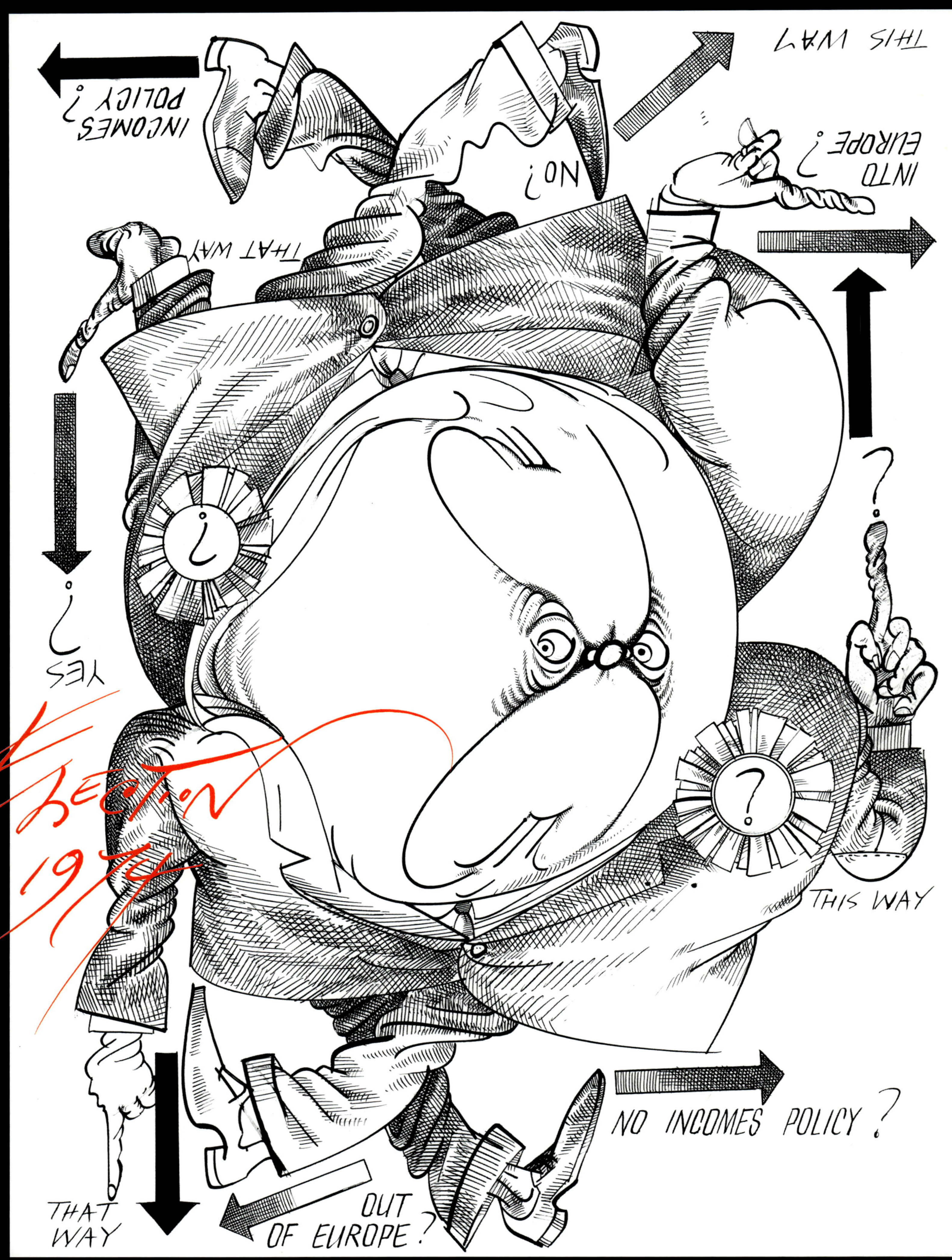
INCOMES POLICY?
NO?
THIS WAY
INTO EUROPE?
THAT WAY
YES?
Election 1974
THIS WAY
NO INCOMES POLICY?
OUT OF EUROPE?
THAT WAY

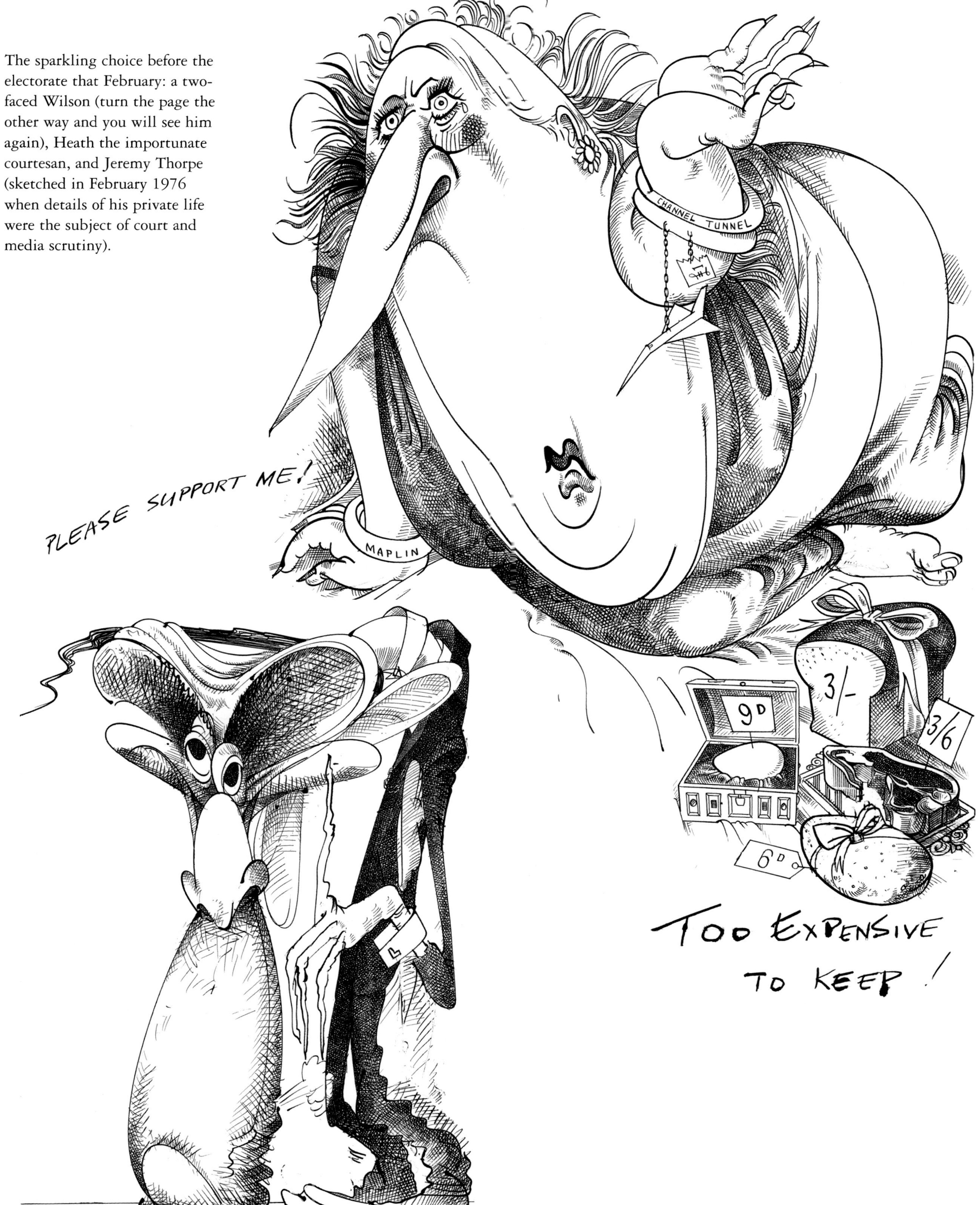

The sparkling choice before the electorate that February: a two-faced Wilson (turn the page the other way and you will see him again), Heath the importunate courtesan, and Jeremy Thorpe (sketched in February 1976 when details of his private life were the subject of court and media scrutiny).

Evel Knievel was a daredevil stuntman who jumped impossible obstacles on his motorbike – but can Evel Wilson do the same? EC referendum day, June 1975.

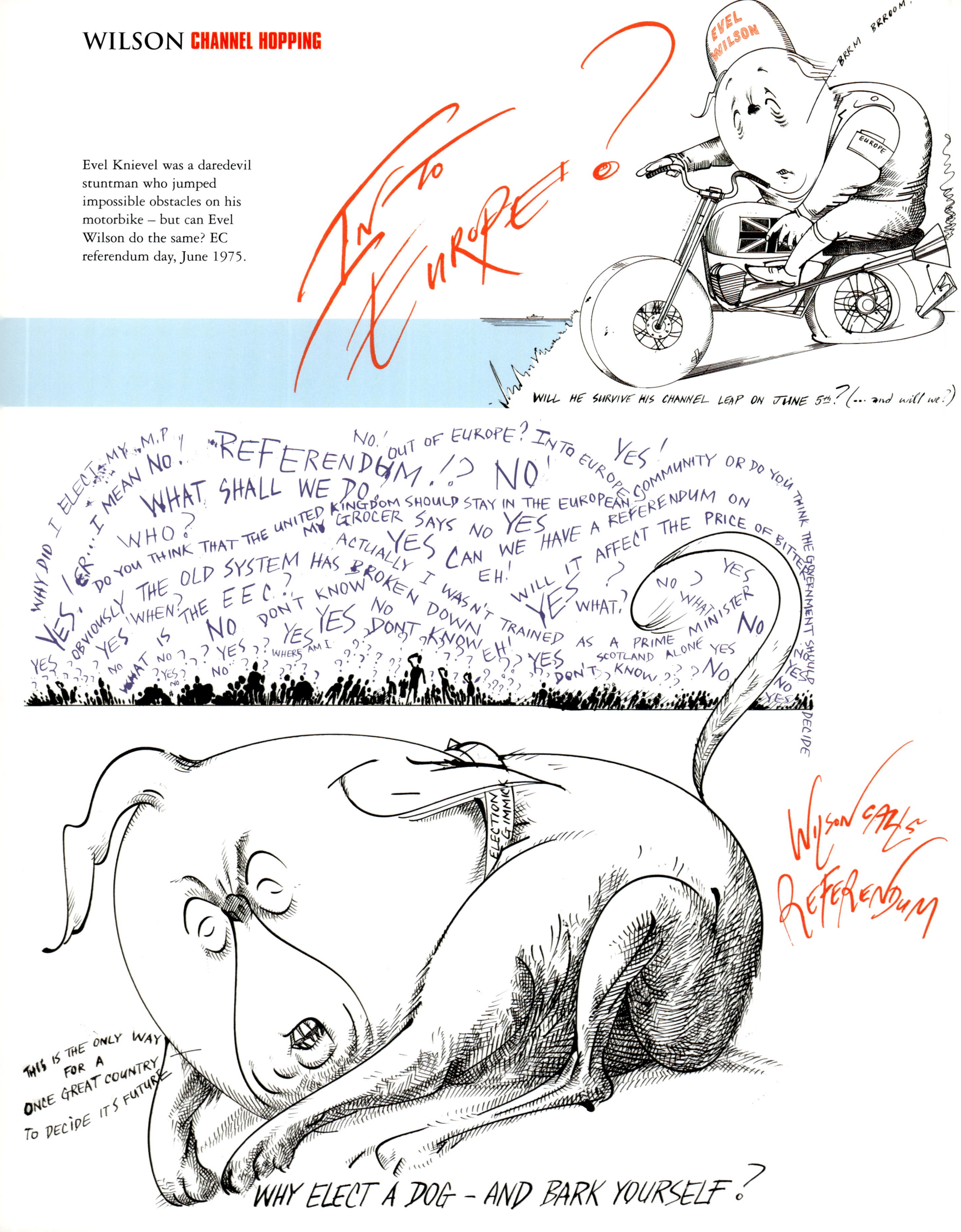

Colourful characters on the issue of Europe: Tony Benn (left), fists up, who voted no in the 1975 referendum; committed pro-European Michael Stewart (top), formerly Wilson's Foreign Secretary; and (bottom), like Benn in opposition, Tory MP Gerald Nabarro and his magnificent handlebar moustaches. Nabarro was once hauled before the court for driving his Rolls-Royce (number plate NAB1) straight over the top of a roundabout. He told the beak his secretary was driving. She took the rap.

(LEFT) December 1969, and President Pompidou of France invites Wilson into the Common Market. The summit in The Hague decided to negotiate Britain's entry into Europe before the summer.

(MAIN PICTURE) Wilson as Groucho Marx, with Trade Secretary Peter Shore as his cigar, outside the EEC Club (January 1975). German chancellor Helmut Schmidt and French president Giscard d'Estaing look on as a pro-European Roy Jenkins grins (in 1977 he accepted the position of President of the European Commission).

I TOLD YOU I ---- ER -- WE WOULD DO WELL IN EUROPE

E.E.C. CLUB.

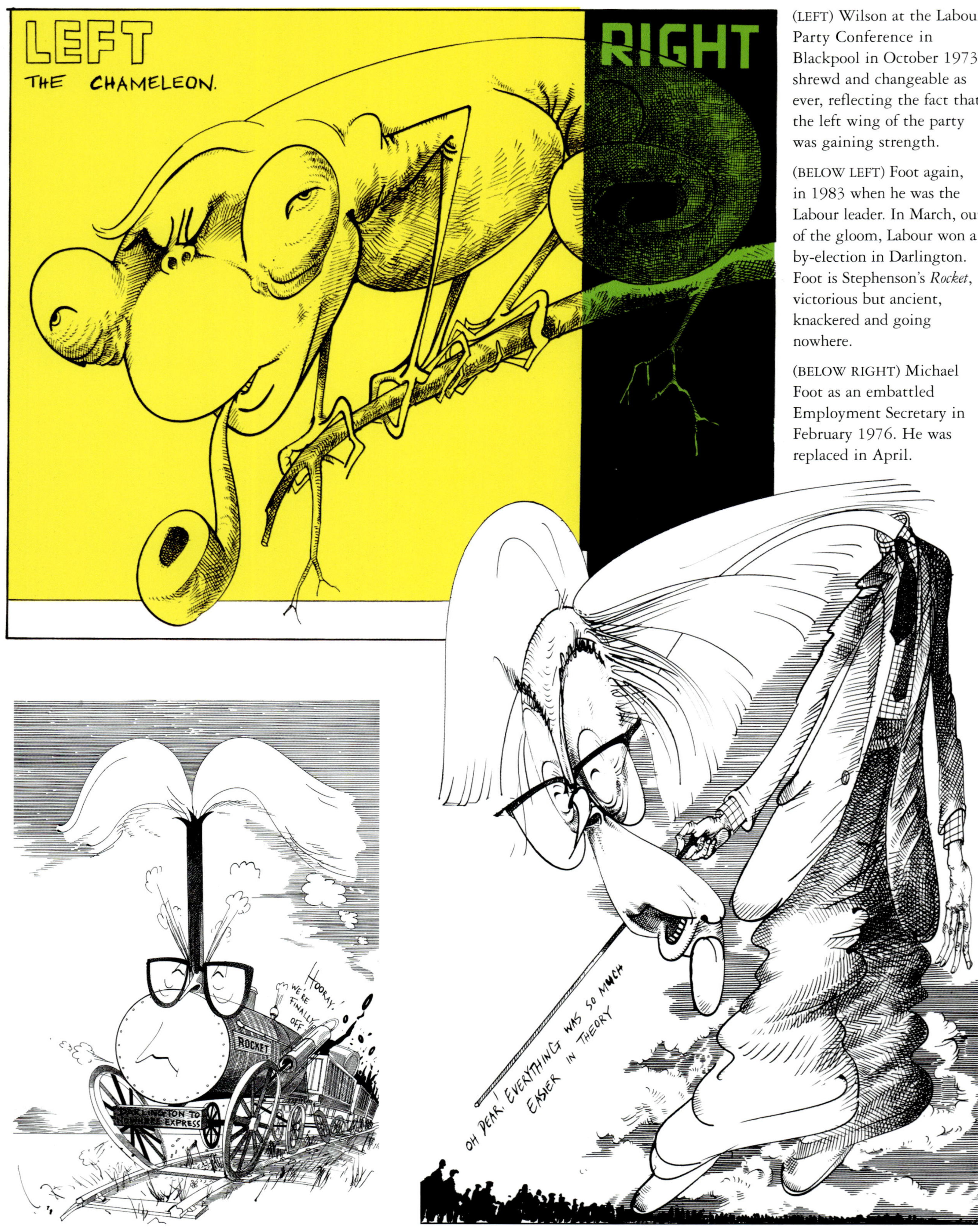

(LEFT) Wilson at the Labour Party Conference in Blackpool in October 1973, shrewd and changeable as ever, reflecting the fact that the left wing of the party was gaining strength.

(BELOW LEFT) Foot again, in 1983 when he was the Labour leader. In March, out of the gloom, Labour won a by-election in Darlington. Foot is Stephenson's *Rocket*, victorious but ancient, knackered and going nowhere.

(BELOW RIGHT) Michael Foot as an embattled Employment Secretary in February 1976. He was replaced in April.

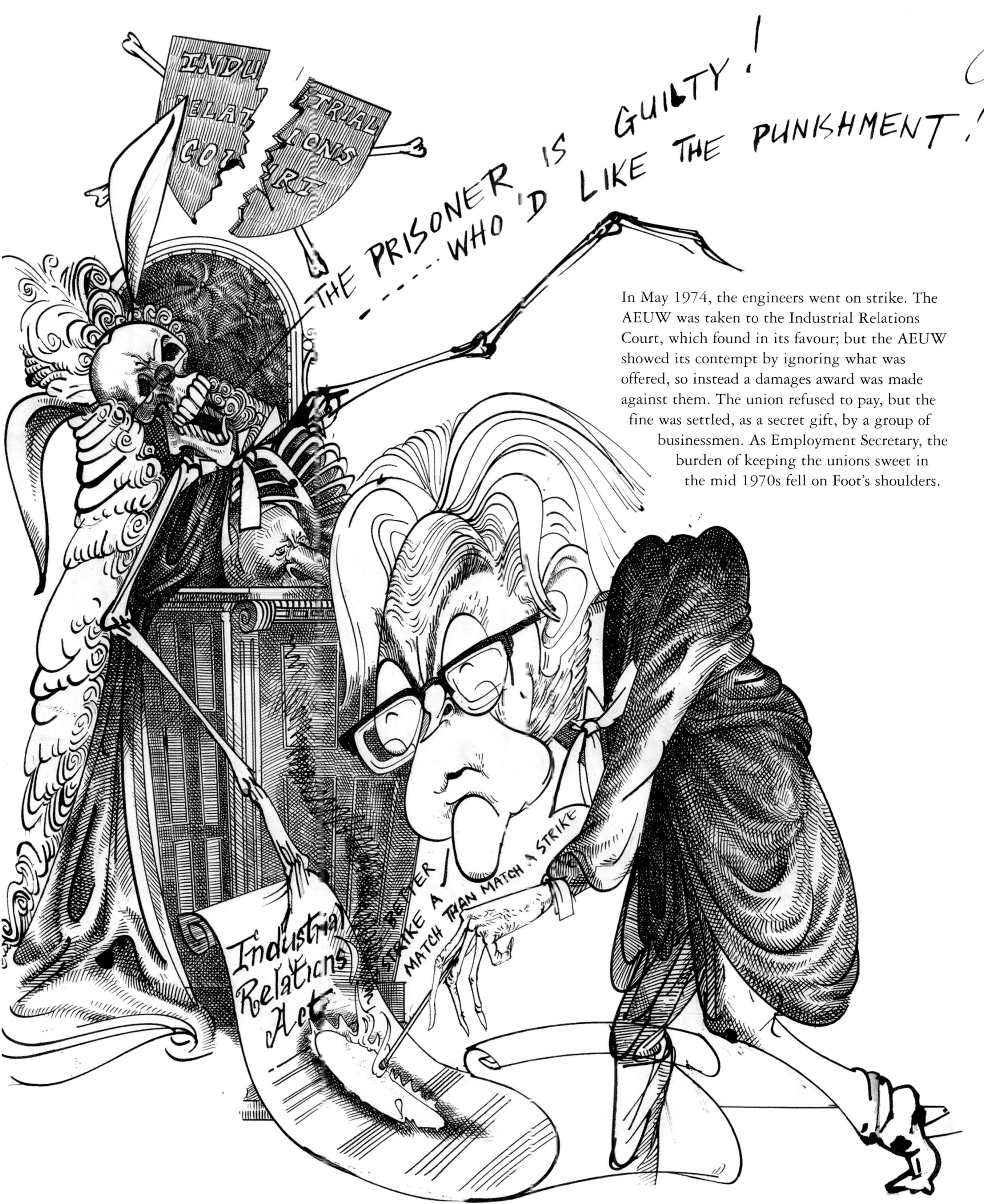

In May 1974, the engineers went on strike. The AEUW was taken to the Industrial Relations Court, which found in its favour; but the AEUW showed its contempt by ignoring what was offered, so instead a damages award was made against them. The union refused to pay, but the fine was settled, as a secret gift, by a group of businessmen. As Employment Secretary, the burden of keeping the unions sweet in the mid 1970s fell on Foot's shoulders.

(TOP) Labour pains. Candidates for the March 1976 leadership contest: Tony Benn, Michael Foot, Jim Callaghan, Roy Jenkins, Anthony Crosland and Denis Healey.

(BELOW) Spring breaks, and the field narrows. Foot had the party's affection, but it was thought he would lose an election. Healey's rugged intellect was admired, but Callaghan was regarded as the most capable.

Marcia Williams, Wilson's private and political secretary, wielded great influence from 1964 to 1970, and was the architect of Labour's election campaign in June 1970 (Labour lost). Wilson caused an honours scandal in 1974 when he made her Baroness Falkender; he himself was knighted in 1976 and created a life peer in 1983

Ian Smith was a very good subject – a malleable rubber face that would stretch in pretty much any direction I wanted it to.

He was a fighter pilot during the war, and he lost an eye. There were those who accused me of drawing him with only one eye, but to be perfectly frank he did only have the one. I considered giving him two, but wouldn't that have been more insulting?

IAN SMITH

PRIME MINISTER OF RHODESIA 1965–1979

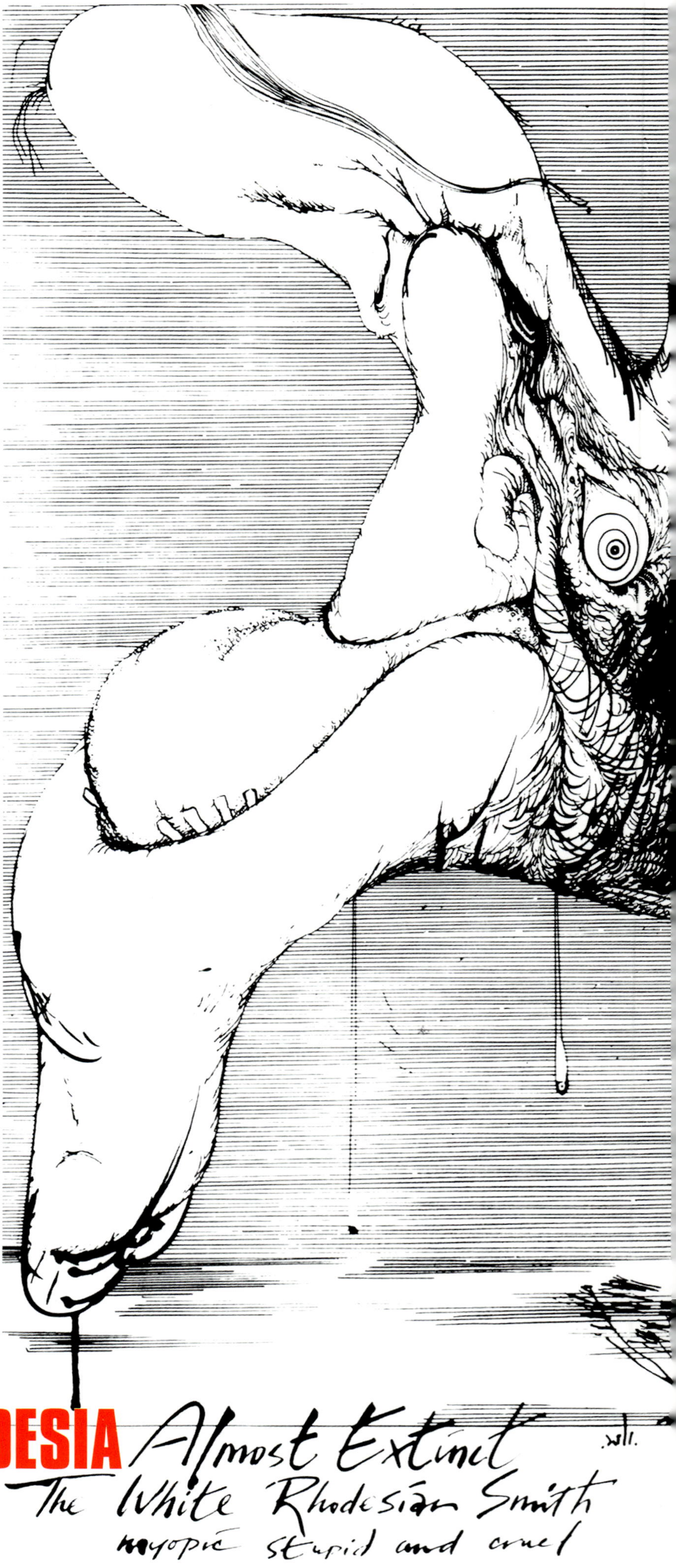

Almost Extinct
The White Rhodesian Smith
myopic stupid and cruel

(OPPOSITE) Kith and kin. Ian Smith sits on the back of a native of Rhodesia while white Rhodesians look on.

(BELOW) Almost Extinct – Ian Smith in the waning years of minority rule in Rhodesia.

(ABOVE) Smith continues to defy Her Majesty's Government with his unilateral declaration of independence (UDI), and to ignore the tidal wave of black resentment.

(BELOW) Henry Kissinger flies away after having negotiated an agreement for majority rule in Rhodesia, leaving Smith rotting in the sun.

The world community had refused to recognise a Rhodesia that had cast itself adrift from Britain and the Commonwealth, and sanctions had been imposed; but it was armed black opposition that eventually wore Smith down and forced him to the negotiating table – a process that ended with the creation of Zimbabwe and the accession to power of Robert Mugabe and his ZANU (PF) party. An evil monster, he was. Eyewitnesses and victims accused him of mass atrocities in Matabeleland in the 1980s. There were tales of torture, killings, people thrown down mineshafts.

IDI AMIN

UGANDAN PRESIDENT 1971–1979

Loathsome man who stole from his people and spent his ill-gotten gains in exile in Saudi Arabia. Kept his opponents' heads in the fridge.

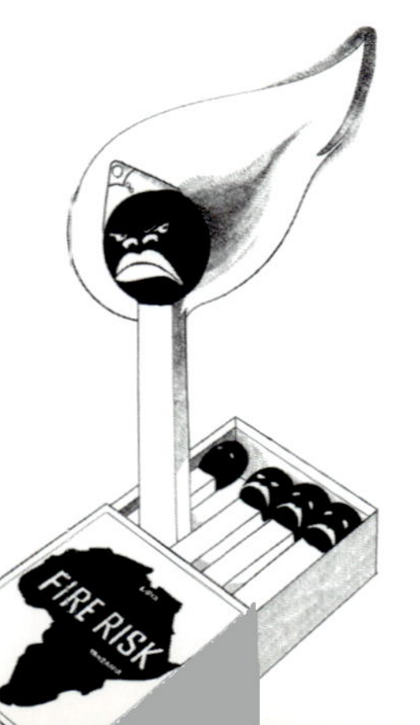

(LEFT) Amin threatens to inflame Africa in 1972.

(RIGHT) 1977, and the activities of Amin, viewed by the rest of the world as a clown, continue to bring cries of atrocity and gross violation of human rights.

RICHARD NIXON

US PRESIDENT 1969–1974

Wow, what a treat. Wonderful gift to my pen. Bony forehead; shifty, baggy eyes under heavy eyebrows; long swooping ski-jump of a nose, below which hung his scrotum-like jowls; six o'clock shadow; glistening with little beads of sweat.

I travelled with Nixon to Cheyenne and beyond, sketching him for *Time* magazine on every occasion. Wherever he gave a speech I was in the front row.

He eventually turned from the monster he was into a squirming, worm, whining, 'You won't have Nixon to kick around any more.'

I was almost sad when he resigned. I would miss him, if only as good raw material. I wrote this little poem on the last cartoon:

'Though Nixon made me sick,
I'll miss his every trick.
His used-car style,
and sweaty smile,
made him a perfect [expletive deleted].'

'People have got to know whether or not their president is a crook. Well, I'm not a crook. I earned everything I've got'

(LEFT) Robert Kennedy and his famous dog Freckles on the campaign trail.

(BELOW) I went to the Miami Republican convention in 1968 and made this drawing for Time magazine. In the foreground, a grinning Nixon stands next to his smug-looking running mate Spiro Agnew, who was later accused of tax fraud.

Nixon campaigning in Los Angeles in June 1968 while Reagan hovers in the background. Below them, Agnew comes down heavily on Vietnam protesters.

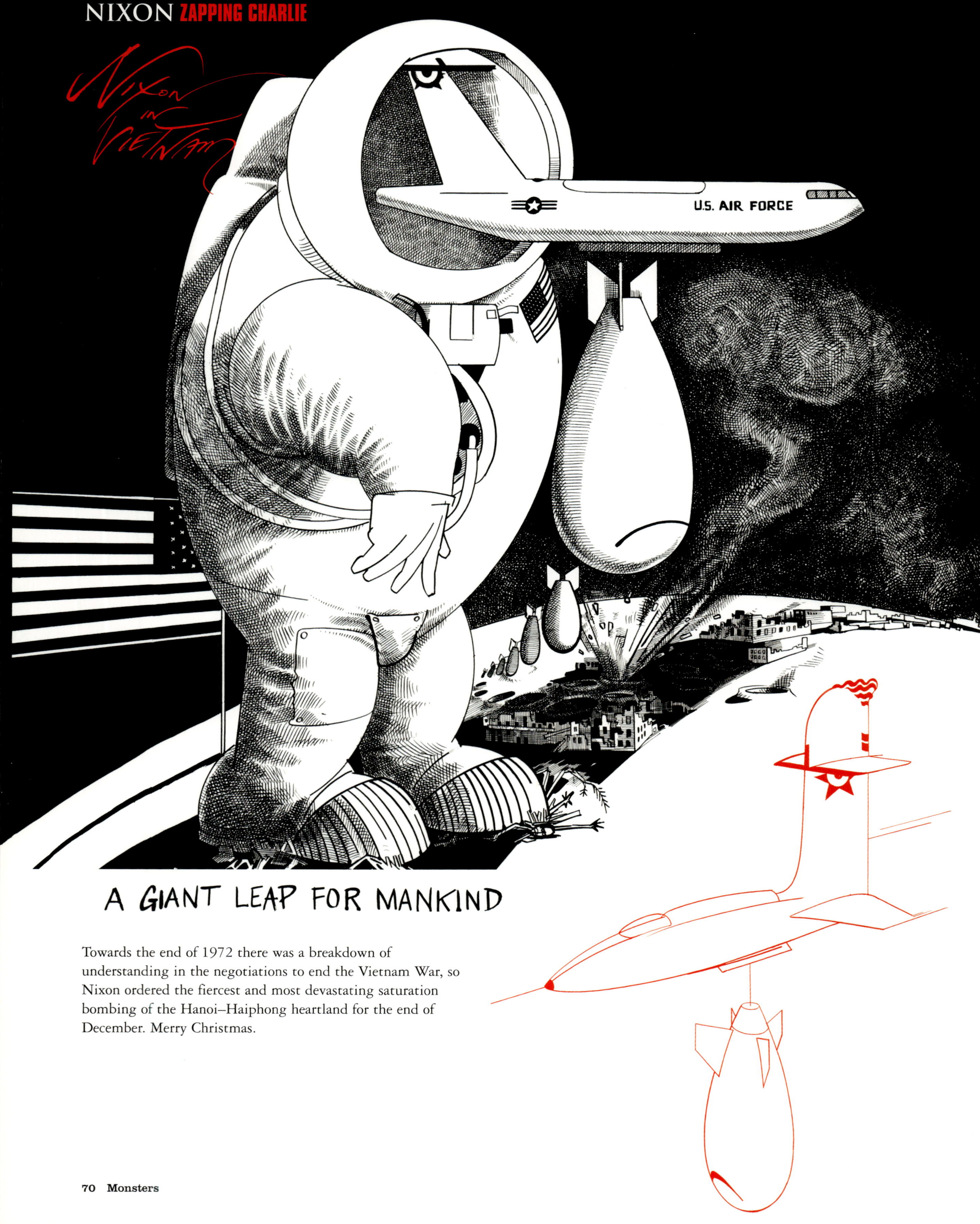

Towards the end of 1972 there was a breakdown of understanding in the negotiations to end the Vietnam War, so Nixon ordered the fiercest and most devastating saturation bombing of the Hanoi–Haiphong heartland for the end of December. Merry Christmas.

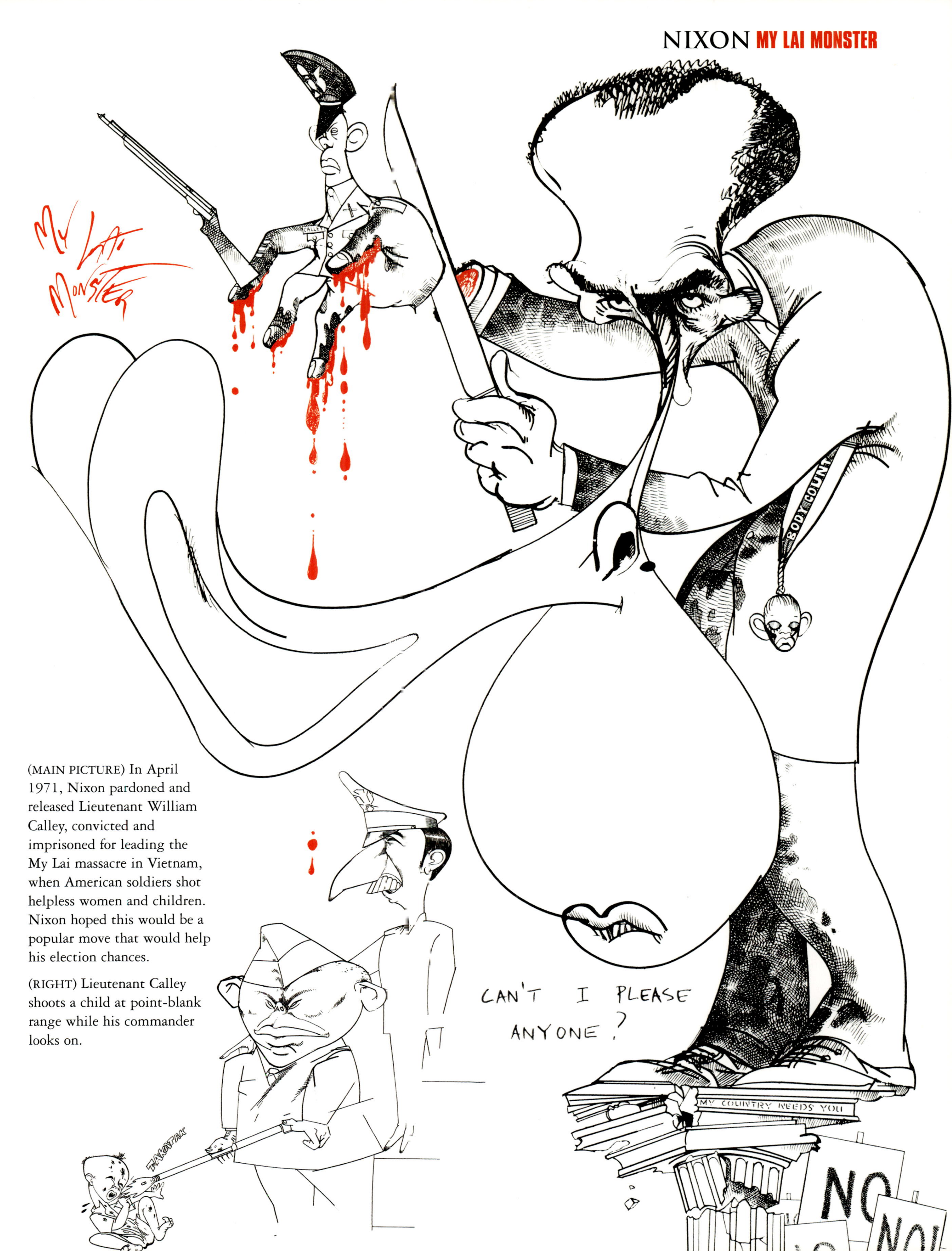

(MAIN PICTURE) In April 1971, Nixon pardoned and released Lieutenant William Calley, convicted and imprisoned for leading the My Lai massacre in Vietnam, when American soldiers shot helpless women and children. Nixon hoped this would be a popular move that would help his election chances.

(RIGHT) Lieutenant Calley shoots a child at point-blank range while his commander looks on.

(MAIN PICTURE) Nixon as the 'Great American War Machine'.

(INSET LEFT) Nixon hiding behind a face mask of his 'flying diplomat' Secretary of State Henry Kissinger; and the children and people of Vietnam drawn on the spot in Saigon.

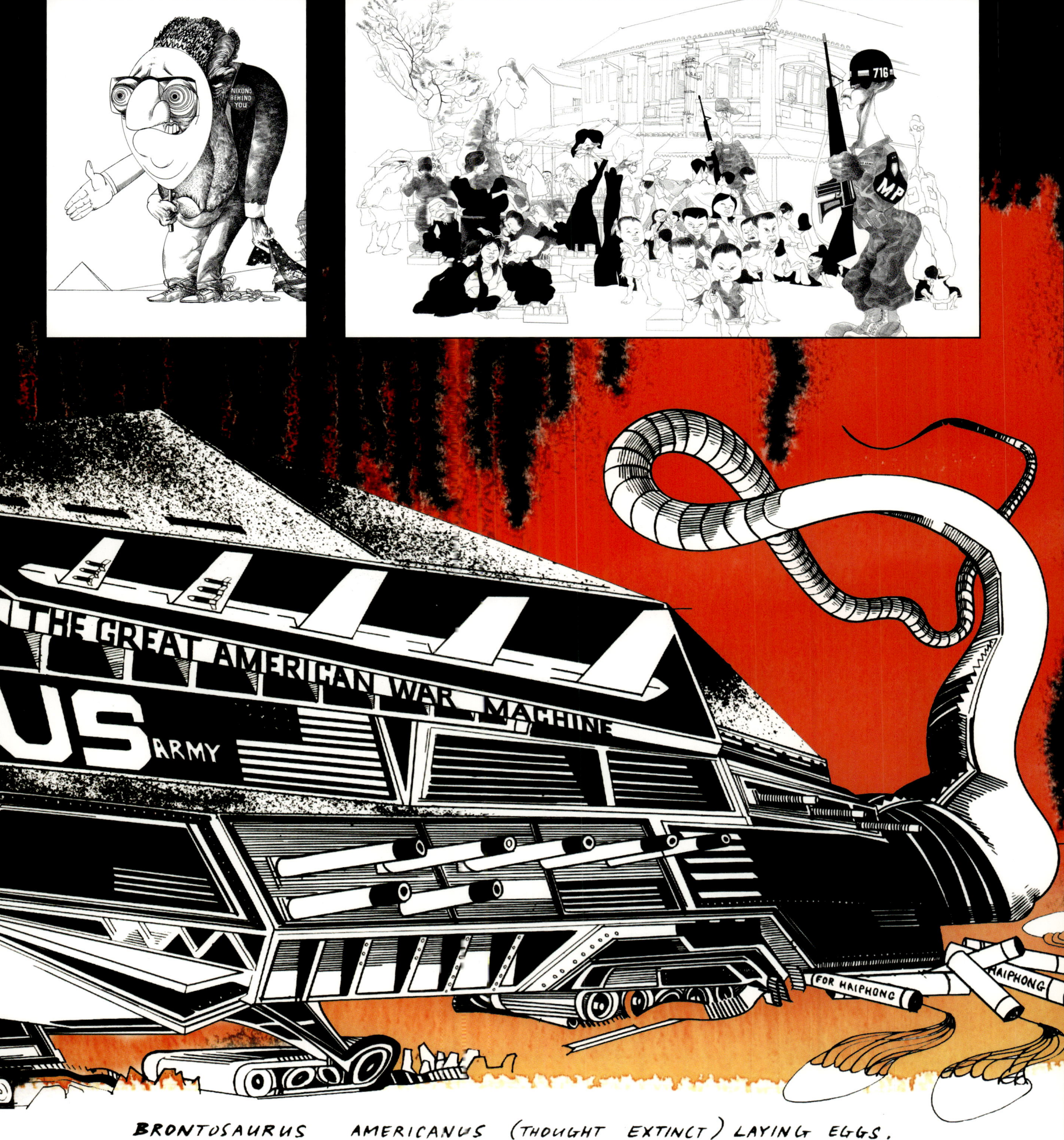

BRONTOSAURUS AMERICANUS (THOUGHT EXTINCT) LAYING EGGS.

Daddy, what did YOU do in the Great War?

(INSET) An American soldier is questioned by his children about his part in the Vietnam War as Nixon (BELOW) announces in good time for the 1972 election that he is going to withdraw from Vietnam.

NIXON'S **NO WHITEWASH AT THE WHITE HOUSE**

By the summer of 1972, Democratic Senator McGovern had emerged as a stronger runner than the Republicans would have wished. In June, some members of the Committee for the Re-election of the President (better known as CREEP) broke into the offices of McGovern's headquarters in the Watergate building, Washington. Nixon denied any knowledge, but former White House lawyer John Dean stated he was ready to testify that Nixon twice joined his aides in discussing a cover-up operation. Top presidential aides John Ehrlichman, Bob Haldeman and John Mitchell (on Nixon's right hand, with Dean) had already resigned.

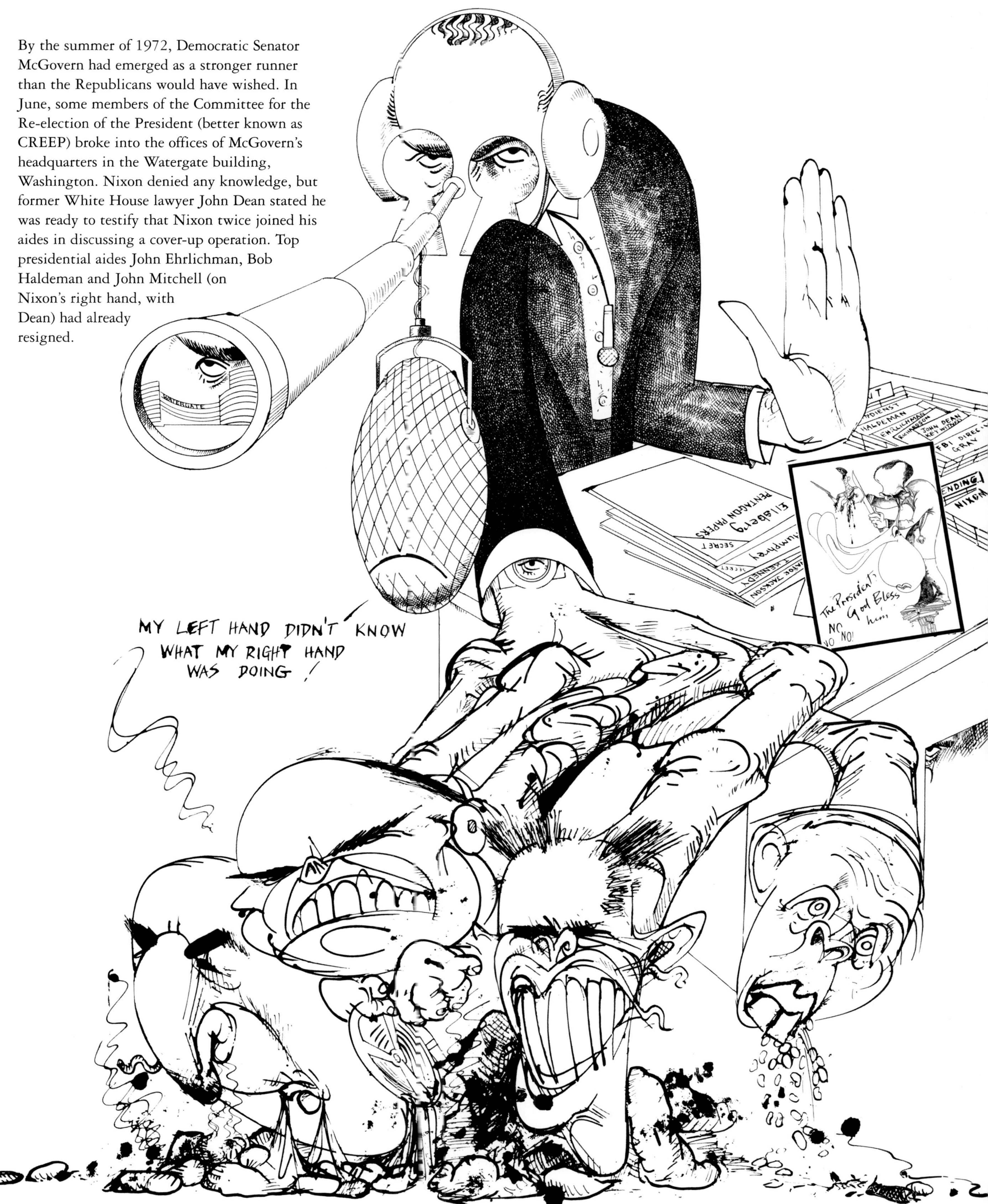

DICKHEAD

(BELOW) The increasingly ridiculous figures of Spiro Agnew and Richard Nixon as Mickey Mouse and Goofy (left); and (right) Nixon in the shape of the Watergate tapes.

(OPPOSITE) By August 1973 the Senate had begun investigating Watergate. The President said he did not know what had happened and refused to give the Senate tape recordings that would prove whether he did or did not, claiming executive privilege. At a press conference in October he tried to pass off Watergate as an irrelevance; he and Brezhnev, who had visited the US in June, were bringing peace to the world, he said. He then ordered a nuclear alert over the USSR and the Middle East. It was suggested that Nixon was playing nuclear games to save his skin.

Ricky Dicky

Watergate

H
GOOD LUCK BREZHNEV
IF I GO,
I'LL TAKE YOU
ALL WITH ME!

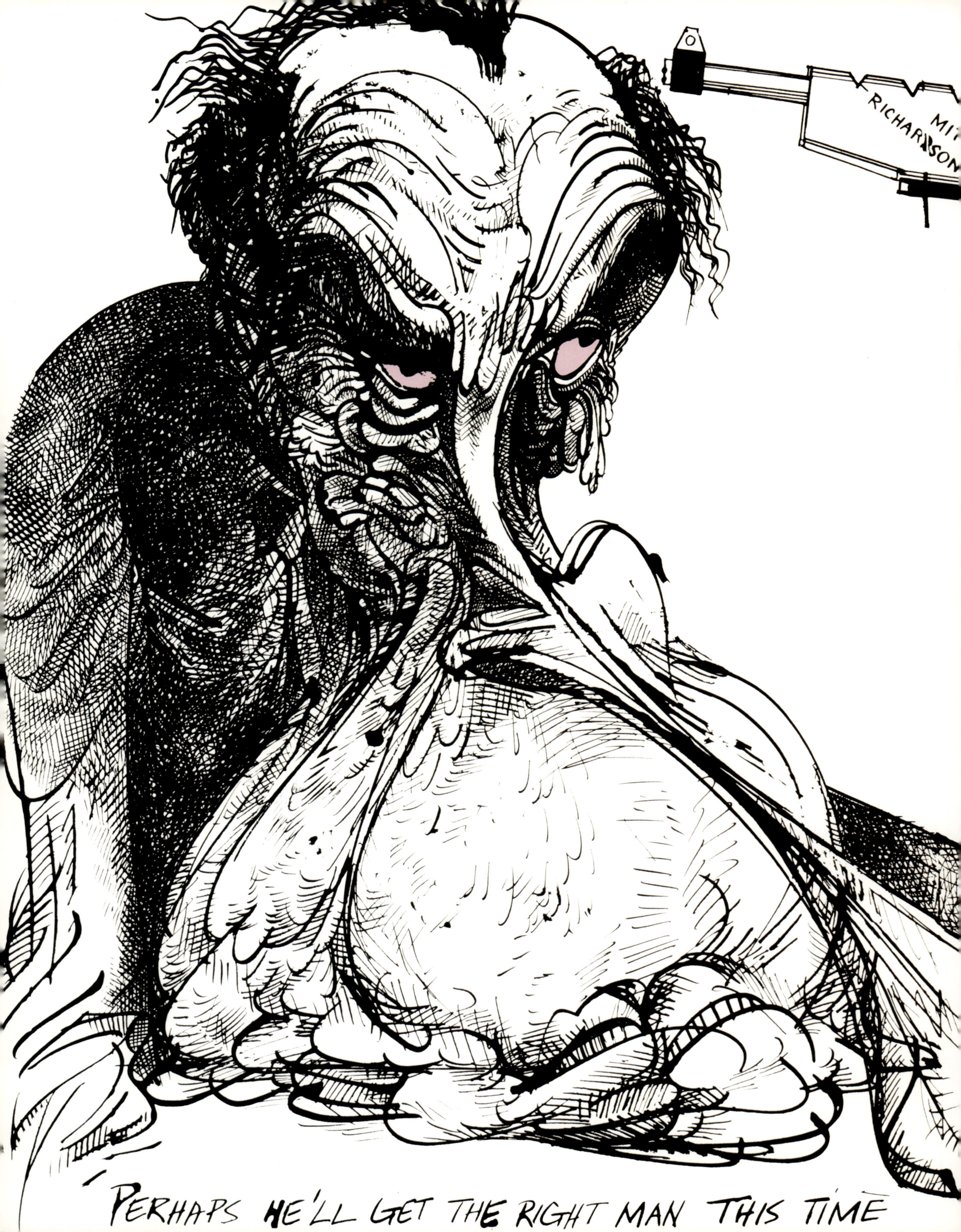
RICHARDSON
PERHAPS HE'LL GET THE RIGHT MAN THIS TIME

As the Watergate affair progressed, Nixon blamed and sacked everyone but himself. In October 1973 came the resignation of Attorney-General Elliot Richardson, who refused to carry out Nixon's order to fire Special Prosecutor Archibald Cox; then came the trials of Haldeman, Ehrlichman and Mitchell. Any corruption attached to previous presidencies was outdistanced by a stretch. In April 1974, the Supreme Court ruled that Nixon must surrender the tapes he held to the Judiciary Committee of the House of Representatives. He handed them over, but parts had been deleted. In July, the committee recommended Nixon's impeachment for obstructing justice and abusing presidential powers, and he finally slouched off to the elephants' graveyard (below).

In August 1974, with two years of his second term left to run, Nixon resigned. He announced his departure in a live television broadcast, claiming amid a haze of sentimental rhetoric, 'As President, I must put the interests of America first.'

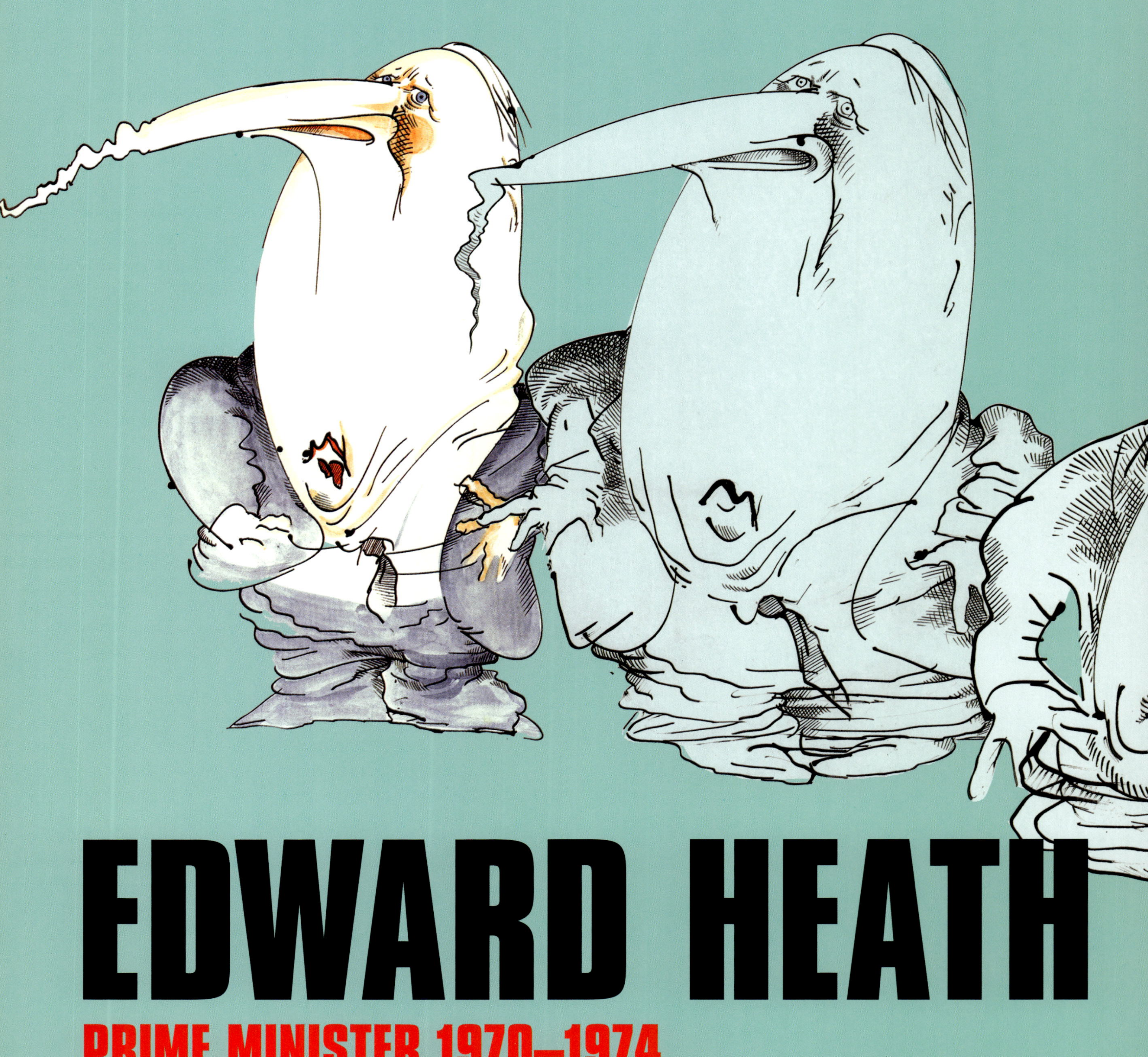

EDWARD HEATH

PRIME MINISTER 1970–1974

Pompous fool; fat and fleshy. I once had lunch with him and others, when I worked at the *Daily Mail* – he was very condescending to me and, I felt, put me down. Bad mistake, for I could never draw him without hearing his plummy voice coming from that petulant rosebud mouth.

Had great fun with his nose. Could stretch it quite a long way and still keep a likeness.

He enjoyed playing his organ and conducting, as well as being an enthusiastic sailor.

Heath in October 1974, now the Leader of the Opposition (and Deflation). His rigidity and misjudgement took the Tories out of office. The 1922 Committee, comprising all Conservative backbench MPs, met to discuss Heath's successor. Would it be Willie Whitelaw, Keith Joseph, Margaret Thatcher, or even chairman of the 1922 Committee Edward du Cann?

'I have no interest in sailing around the world. Not that there is any lack of requests for me to do so'

Heath, a keen sailor, and his boat *Morning Cloud* in the summer of 1971 – while Clydeside shipbuilders were out of work. There was public anger over this, and over 30 million pounds of taxpayers' money was pumped into the Upper Clyde Shipbuilders consortium, to no avail.

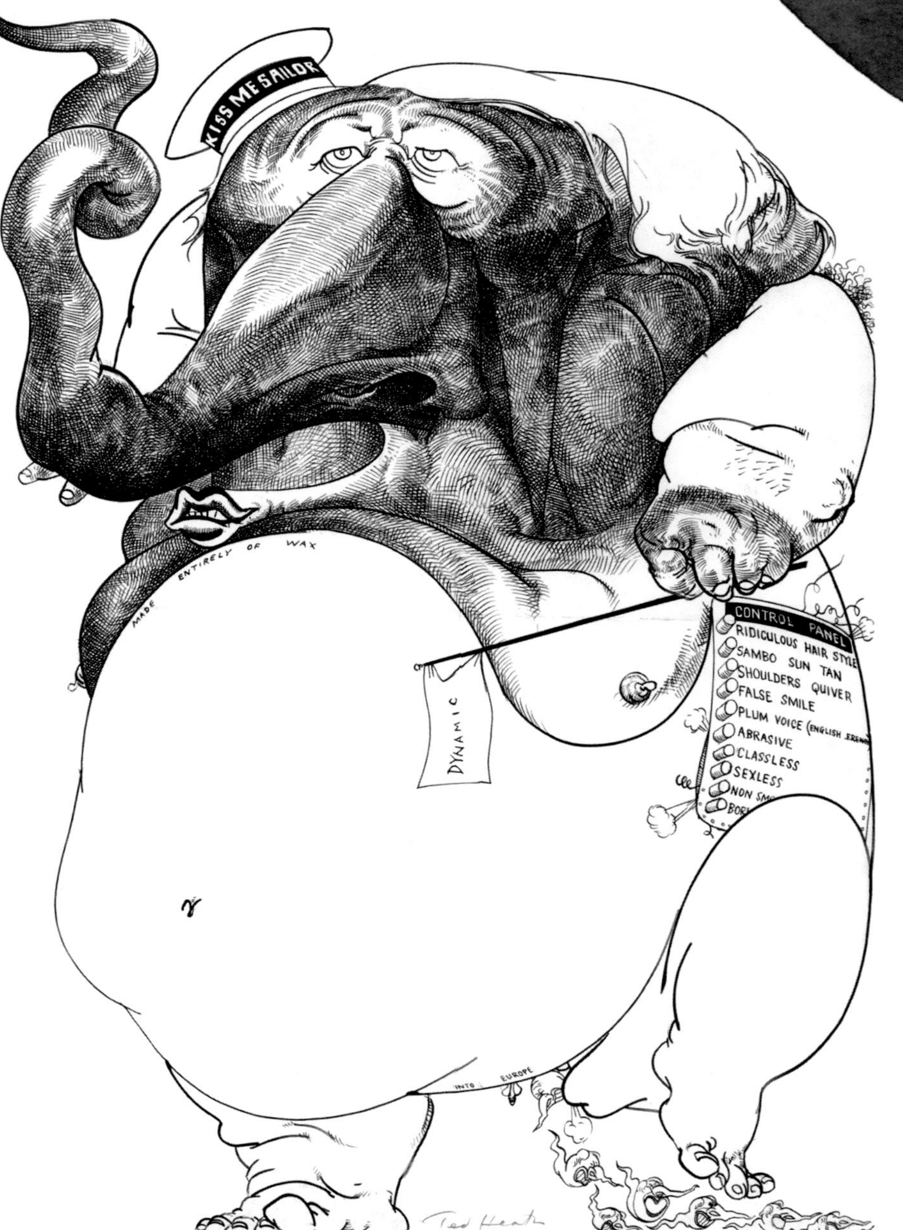

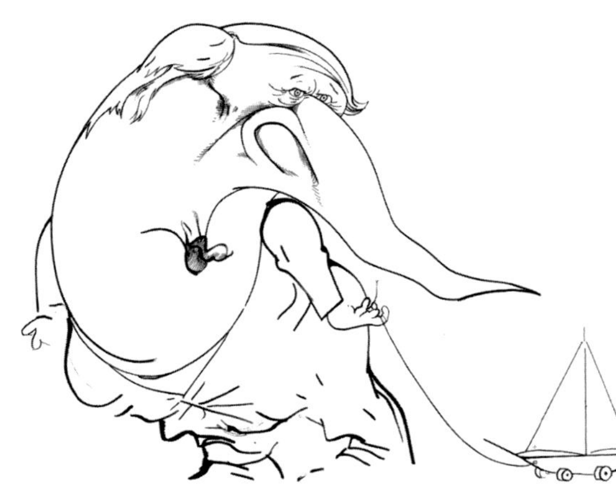

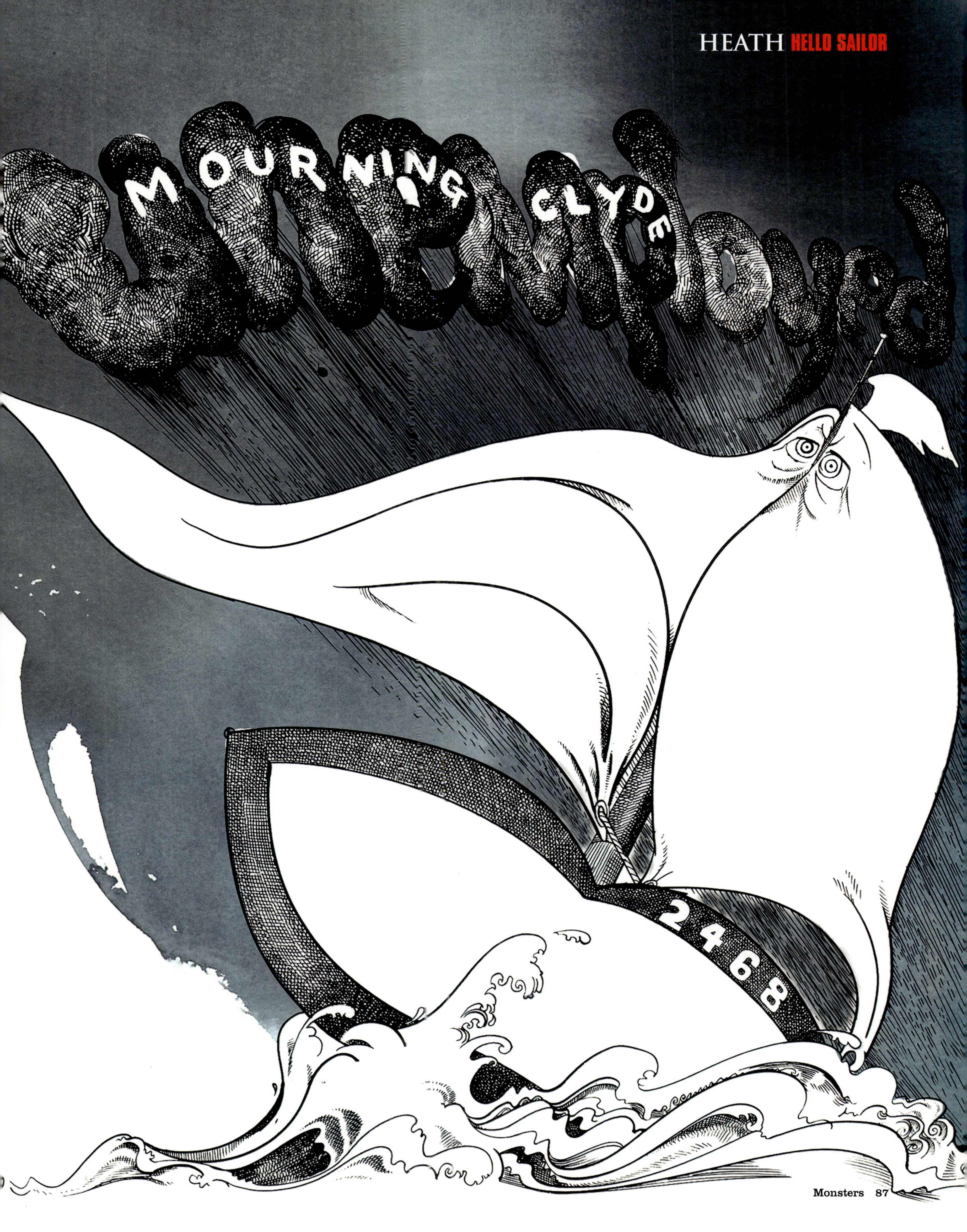
MOURNING CLYDE
2468

(ABOVE, clockwise from top) Edward Heath, Iain Macleod (for a month Heath's Chancellor), Alec Douglas-Home (Foreign Secretary), Selwyn Lloyd (Speaker of the House of Commons from 1971) and Quintin Hogg (Lord Chancellor).

(OPPOSITE) A poster for the Conservative Party in November 1970, inspired by a Tory poster that called Labour 'Yesterday's Men'. 'The Day Before Yesterday's Men' featured new PM Edward Heath (riding bareback on Joe Public) and (top to bottom) Alec Douglas-Home, Anthony Barber (the newly installed Chancellor), John Davies (Trade and Industry) and Robert Carr, the Employment Secretary, with a striker in his talons.

PHUT!
New Tory Image
YES! IT'S THE ~~NEW~~ OLD TORIES AGAIN
WELL WHAT DID YOU EXPECT
STRIKE!

HEATH **OUT OF GAS**

Record interest rates, oil and coal crises, continuing balance of payments shock, petrol shortages . . . the Yom Kippur War left the Israelis in a strong position in the Middle East. In November 1973 Saudi Arabia imposed an oil embargo as a political weapon aimed at the US in the hope that Nixon would coax the Israelis into making concessions. A clockwork Heath marches relentlessly on . . .

In August 1971, the PM of Ireland, Jack Lynch, attacked Heath over the Ulster internment programme.

Edward Heath and his comic opera in three industrial relations acts (July 1972). The acts gave individuals new rights to belong to trade unions if they wished, and to be compensated for unfair dismissal. It gave unions new chances to recruit and win recognition from hostile employers. It gave the government the opportunity to intervene in strikes that were damaging to society.

The Queen of Hearts. By the summer of 1972 the smell of failure and farce had begun to surround the government. The Industrial Relations Court failed to make the government's contempt writ against five shop stewards stick under the provisions of the Industrial Relations Act, even after summoning up the High Court tipstaff and the official solicitor. The government's stand was weakened by public sympathy for the striking dockers, who were seen as an underpaid group.

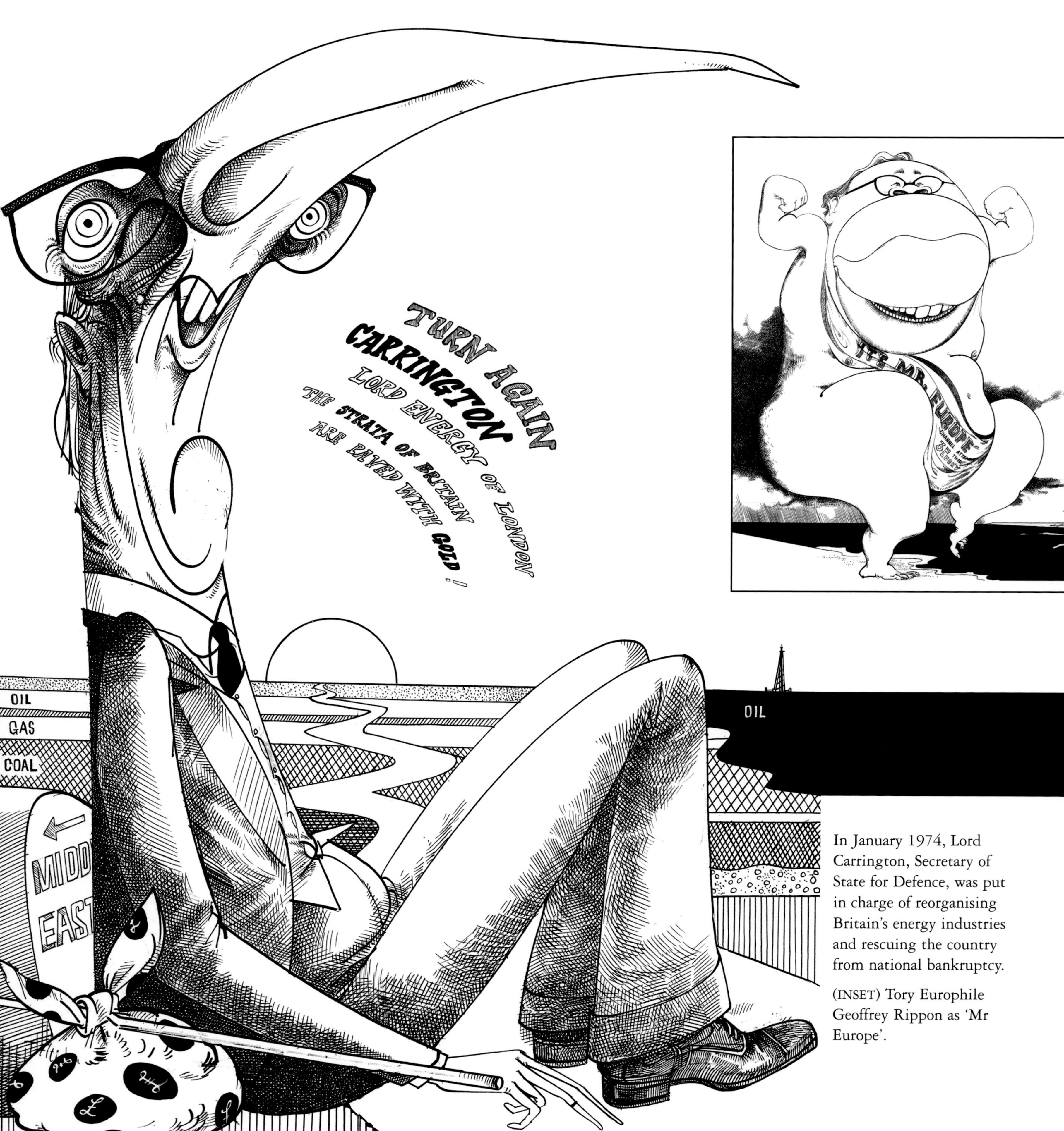

In January 1974, Lord Carrington, Secretary of State for Defence, was put in charge of reorganising Britain's energy industries and rescuing the country from national bankruptcy.

(INSET) Tory Europhile Geoffrey Rippon as 'Mr Europe'.

(TOP) Heath and Pompidou. Hands across the water.

(ABOVE) A coat of arms for Britain and France, together in Europe: the Heath lion and the Pompidou cockerel. It's all in the details.

(RIGHT) Heath met President Pompidou in Paris in May 1971. It was feared that Britain would come off worse when she joined the Common Market. There were difficulties over sugar, New Zealand butter and other housekeeping details.

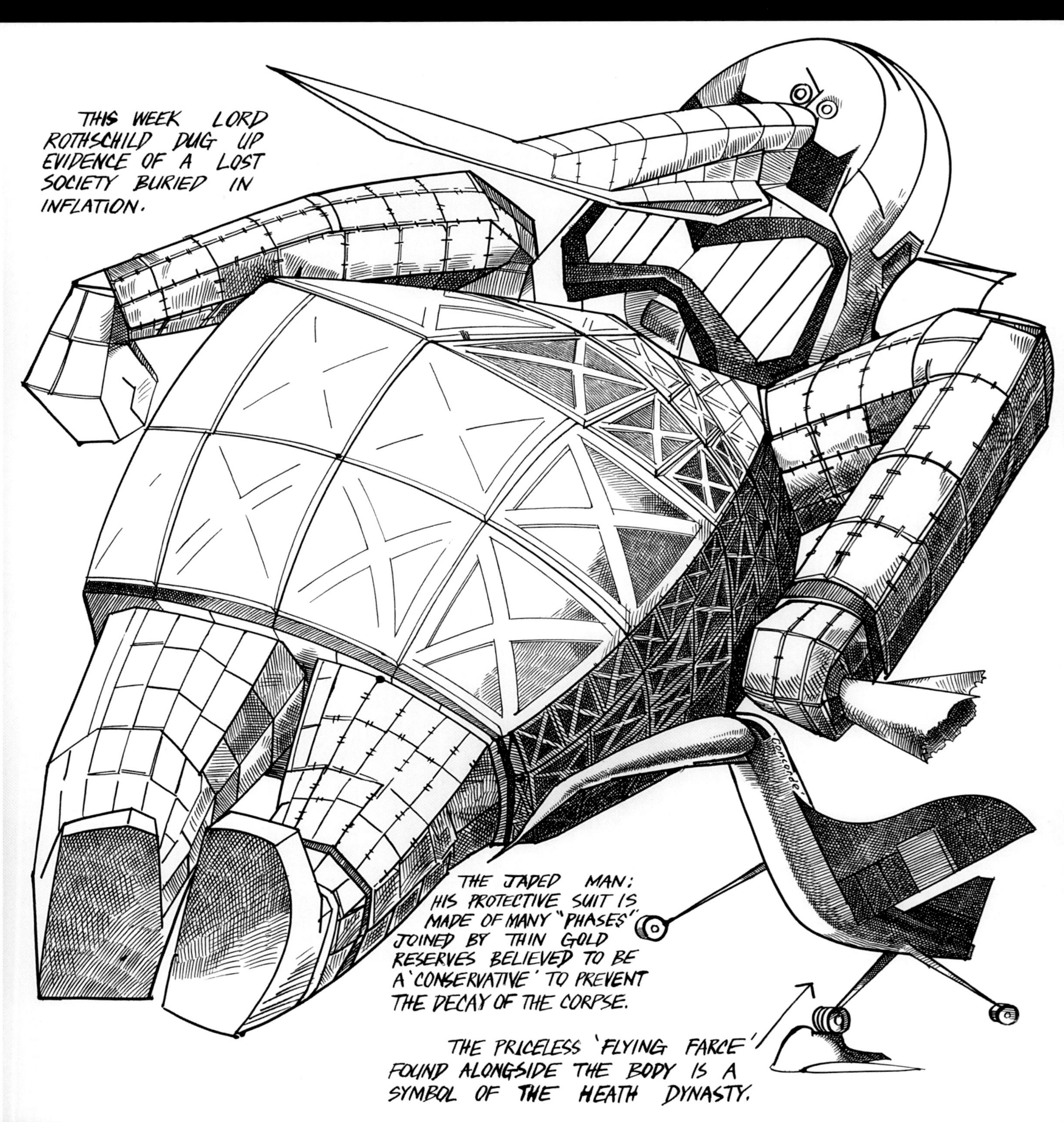

Edward Heath as the Amazing Jaded Man in the autumn of 1973, when the Genius of China exhibition (archaeological finds from the People's Republic of China) was being held at the Royal Academy. The 'Flying Farce' is Concorde, regarded by some as a monstrously expensive folly.

Christmas 1973, and a Churchillian Heath soldiers on despite the coal strike and the power crisis bringing British industry to the brink of chaos. Heath ordered a three-day working week, which was viewed with foreboding by industrialists who feared major economic damage to the country. The railwaymen, under General Secretary Sidney Weighell, worked to rule. In the miners' dispute, the government suggested that the miners be paid for waiting time. On the right (clockwise) are Anthony Barber, Geoffrey Rippon and William Whitelaw.

HATRED

Reflections on the persistent rivalry between Heath and Thatcher.

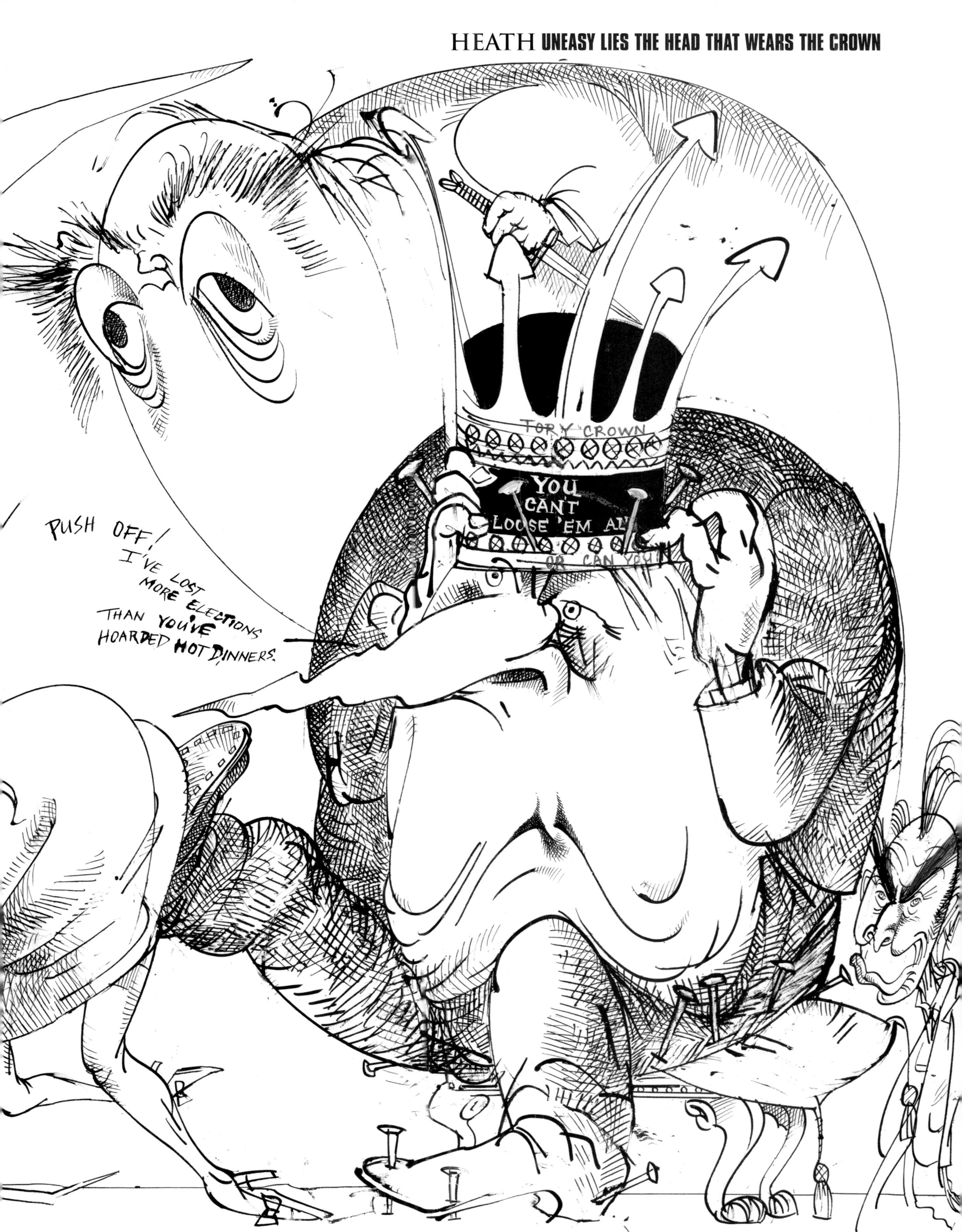
TORY CROWN
YOU CAN'T LOOSE 'EM AL
OR CAN YOU
PUSH OFF! I'VE LOST MORE ELECTIONS THAN YOU'VE HOARDED HOT DINNERS.

After leaving office, Heath retired to the Close at Salisbury Cathedral and concentrated on conducting and playing his organ.

Heath's beloved *Morning Cloud* lies beached and broken as Wilson and his Labour Party take up the reins of power once more at the end of 1974.

ENOCH POWELL

Enoch Powell's mad staring eyes, fleshy lips and racist attacks inspired me to more and more grotesqueries. One of the cleverest minds in politics, he was a thorn in the side of the Conservative Party, defying Mr Heath and remaining stridently anti-Common Market.

ivers of Bloo

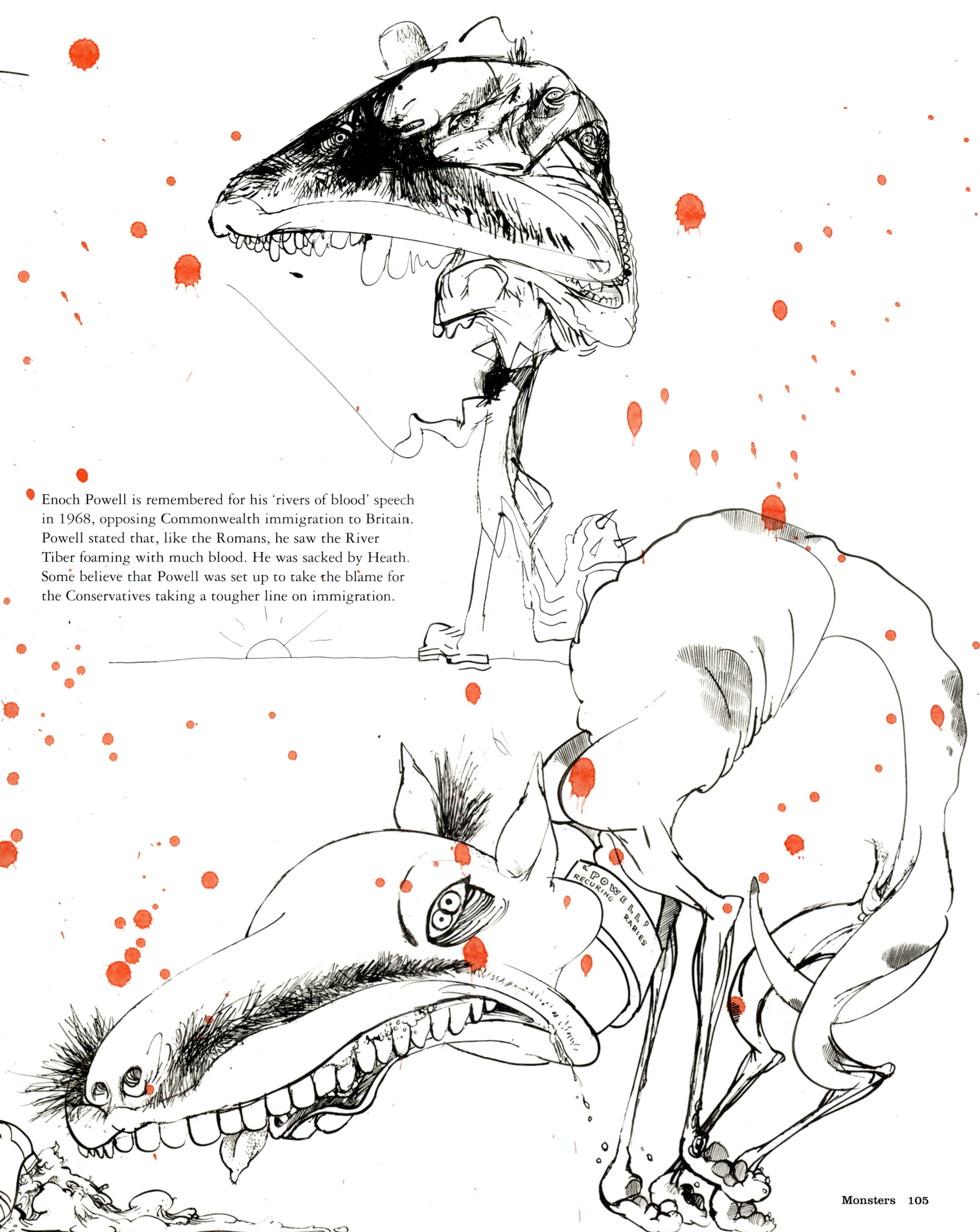

Enoch Powell is remembered for his 'rivers of blood' speech in 1968, opposing Commonwealth immigration to Britain. Powell stated that, like the Romans, he saw the River Tiber foaming with much blood. He was sacked by Heath. Some believe that Powell was set up to take the blame for the Conservatives taking a tougher line on immigration.

Building Monsters
Bigotry and Violence

NORTHERN IRELAND

(OPPOSITE) The Reverend Ian Paisley (Democratic Unionist Party) thunders from the pulpit at a supremely unagitated Gerry Adams (Sinn Fein) while behind them Northern Ireland explodes and crosses continue to be erected.

In July 1970, large numbers of British troops sealed off the Falls Road area in Belfast to search house-to-house for Nationalist weapons. Initially, most Nationalists were happy to see the arrival of the British Army, but this was a major turning point.

GERALD FORD

US PRESIDENT 1974-1977

'I've had a lot of experience with people smarter than I am'

Gerald Ford – well, as a monster, Nixon was a hard act to follow, and Ford couldn't cut the mustard. He fell into the job when his boss resigned. He was as thick as two planks and I drew him as a blank, bland moon face, with close-set eyes and plenty of teeth.

In September 1974, Ford granted Nixon a full, free and absolute pardon. Some defended the decision, arguing that Nixon's abuses of power were rooted in American history; others called it an error of judgement.

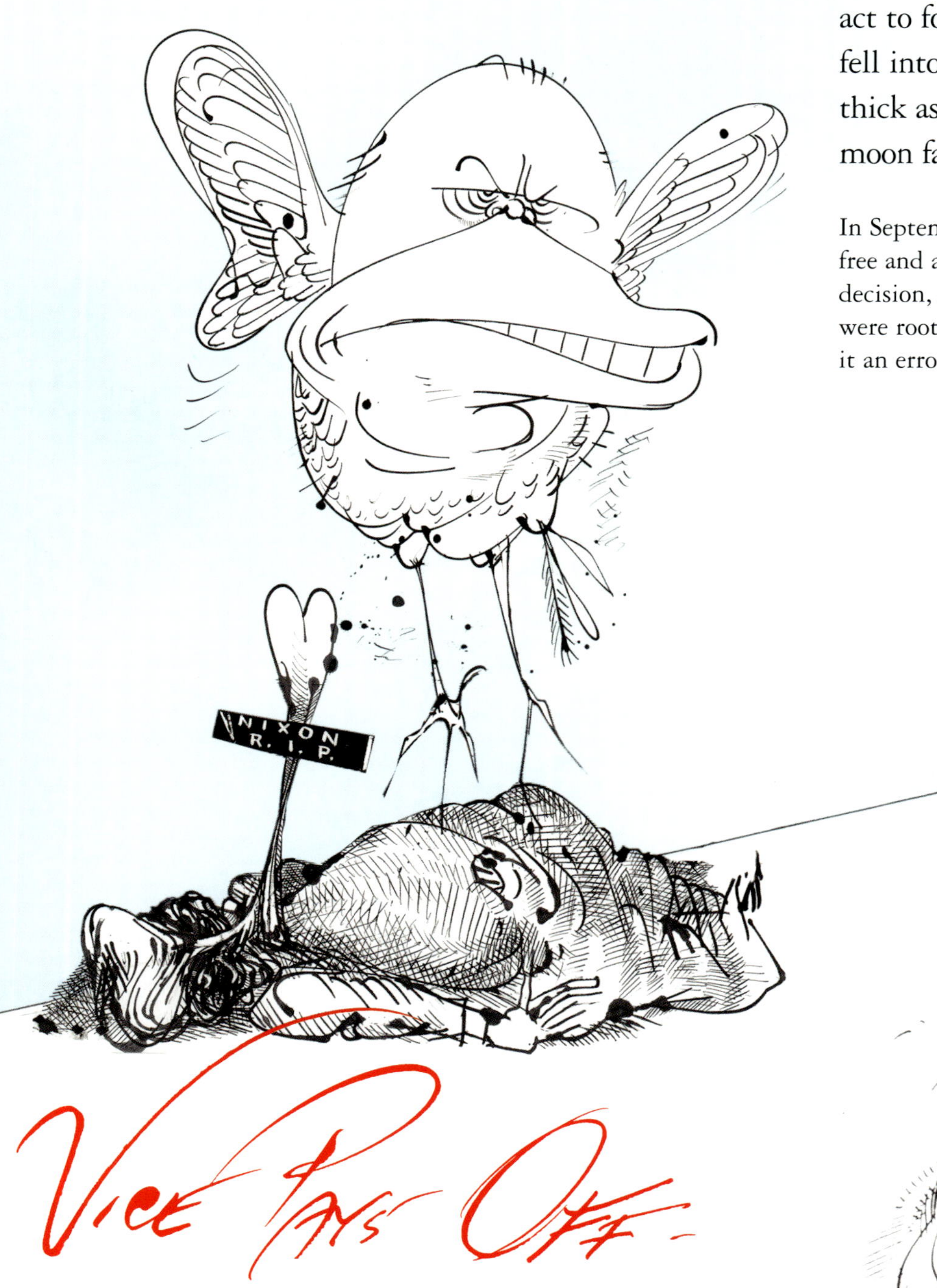

THE GOOD FORD WILL PARDON U.S. ALL

The race for the White House in 1976. Ford was felt by the public not to be truly in charge of foreign and defence policies. In order to enforce his authority and gain some respect, he engineered a Cabinet shake-up, but mishandled it (right). While he slugged it out with presidential hopeful Ronald Reagan (left), Jimmy Carter (the 'Georgia Cat') gained ground with amazing speed.

COULDN'T CHEW GUM AND WALK AT THE SAME TIME.
NOW WILL YOU TAKE ME SERIOUSLY?

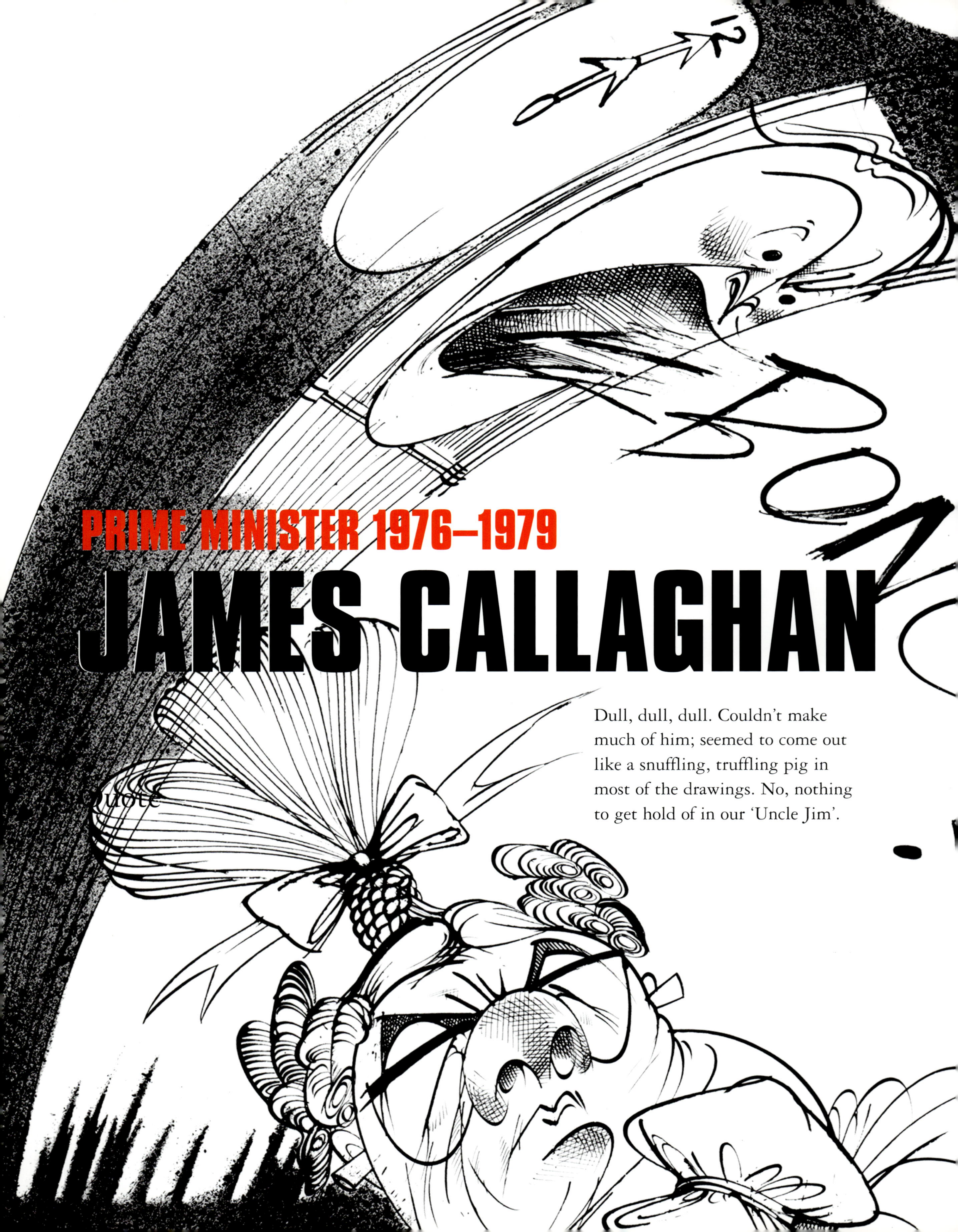

PRIME MINISTER 1976–1979

JAMES CALLAGHAN

Dull, dull, dull. Couldn't make much of him; seemed to come out like a snuffling, truffling pig in most of the drawings. No, nothing to get hold of in our 'Uncle Jim'.

Tony Benn, calling time on a leader he felt had steered Labour too far to the right. He talked of re-founding the party and becoming its next leader, which prompted a 'Stop Benn' campaign.

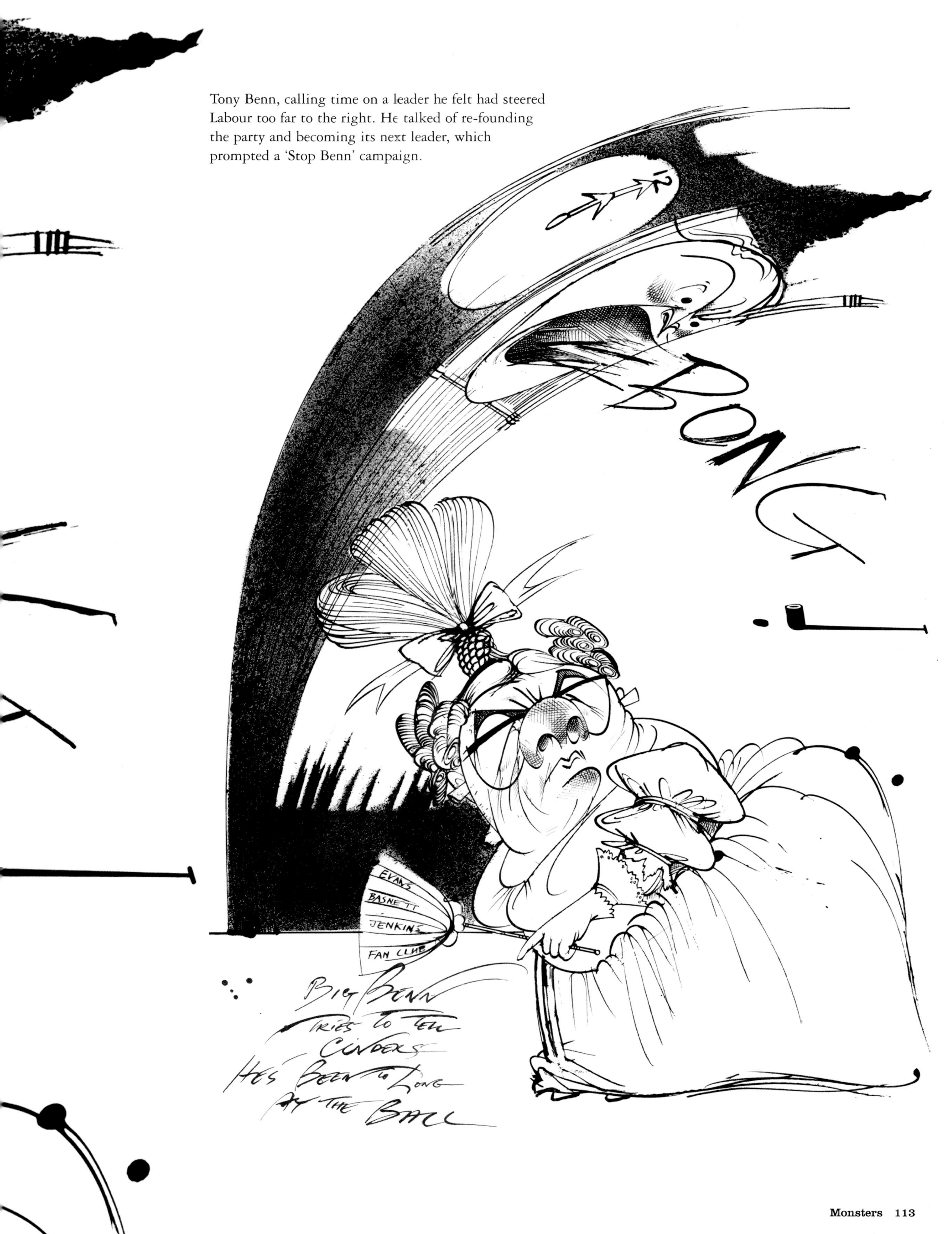

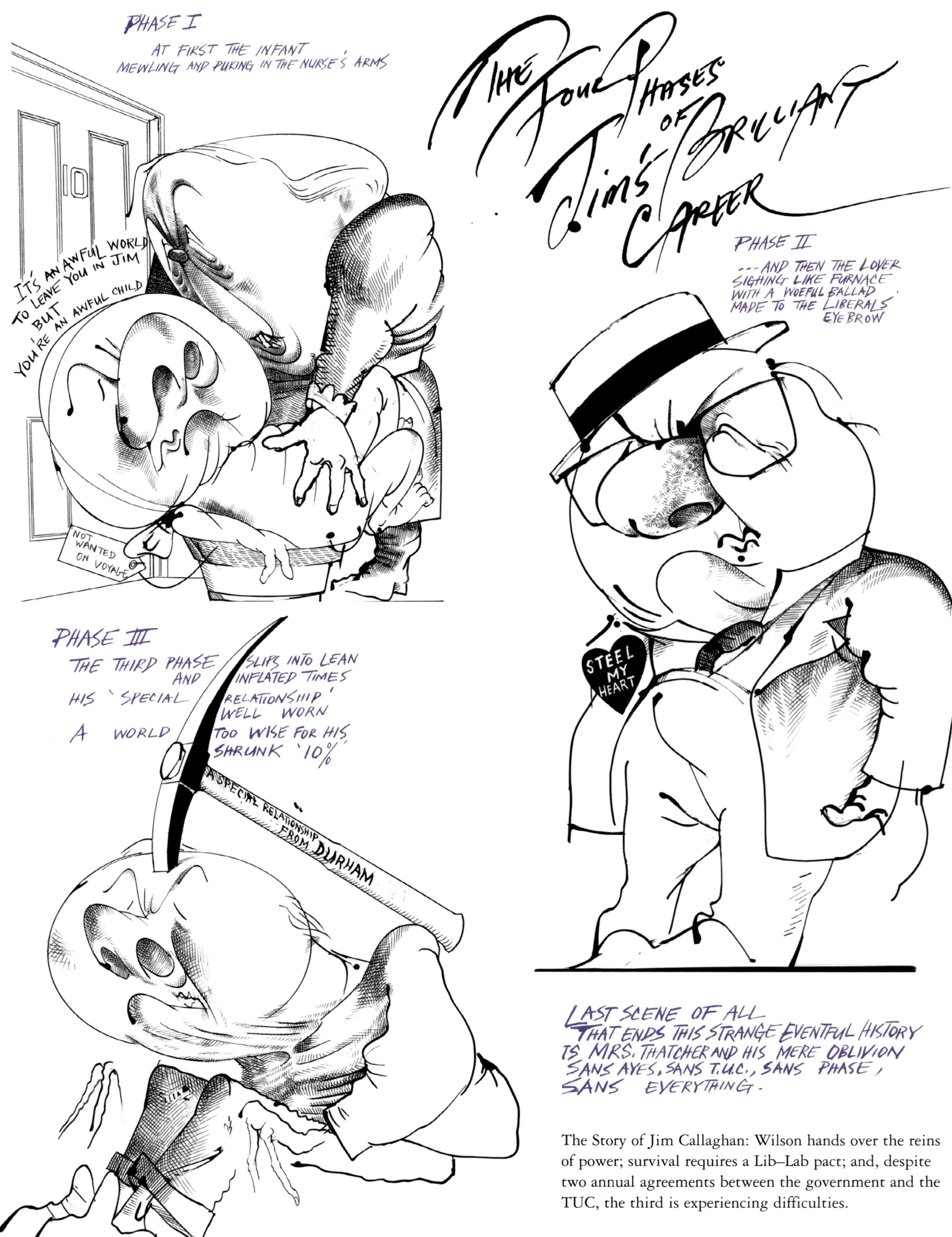

The Story of Jim Callaghan: Wilson hands over the reins of power; survival requires a Lib–Lab pact; and, despite two annual agreements between the government and the TUC, the third is experiencing difficulties.

A tremulous David Steel rides on Callaghan's porcine rump as Leader of the Opposition Margaret Thatcher, expecting an imminent election given the government's appalling record, harangues from her perch.

E.E.C. OR BUST!
THE GANG OF FOUR

DR DAVID OWEN

Yet another Oxbridge politician, and a fully qualified doctor to boot, Dr Owen suffered from a haughty tone and demeanour. I felt this, and his lack of political weight, to be a disadvantage – about as disadvantageous as going into battle with the Thatcher dalek armed with an umbrella.

(LEFT) In 1981, Dr David Owen was one of the so-called 'Gang of Four' that broke away from the Labour Party to found the Social Democratic Party (SDP), a left-of-centre movement hoping to seize the middle ground. To the left are fellow gang members Shirley Williams and Roy Jenkins, and on the right is a craggy Bill Rodgers.

SHINGTON
ROOSEVELT
LINCOLN

JIMMY CARTER

US PRESIDENT 1977–1981

What a dullard was Carter. Good man, Christian and all that, but ineffective – I should say so. Crisis after crisis. Maybe he was too nice. Maybe to be a leader you have to be a nasty tough bastard, but not Carter. Bland in office, bland to draw.

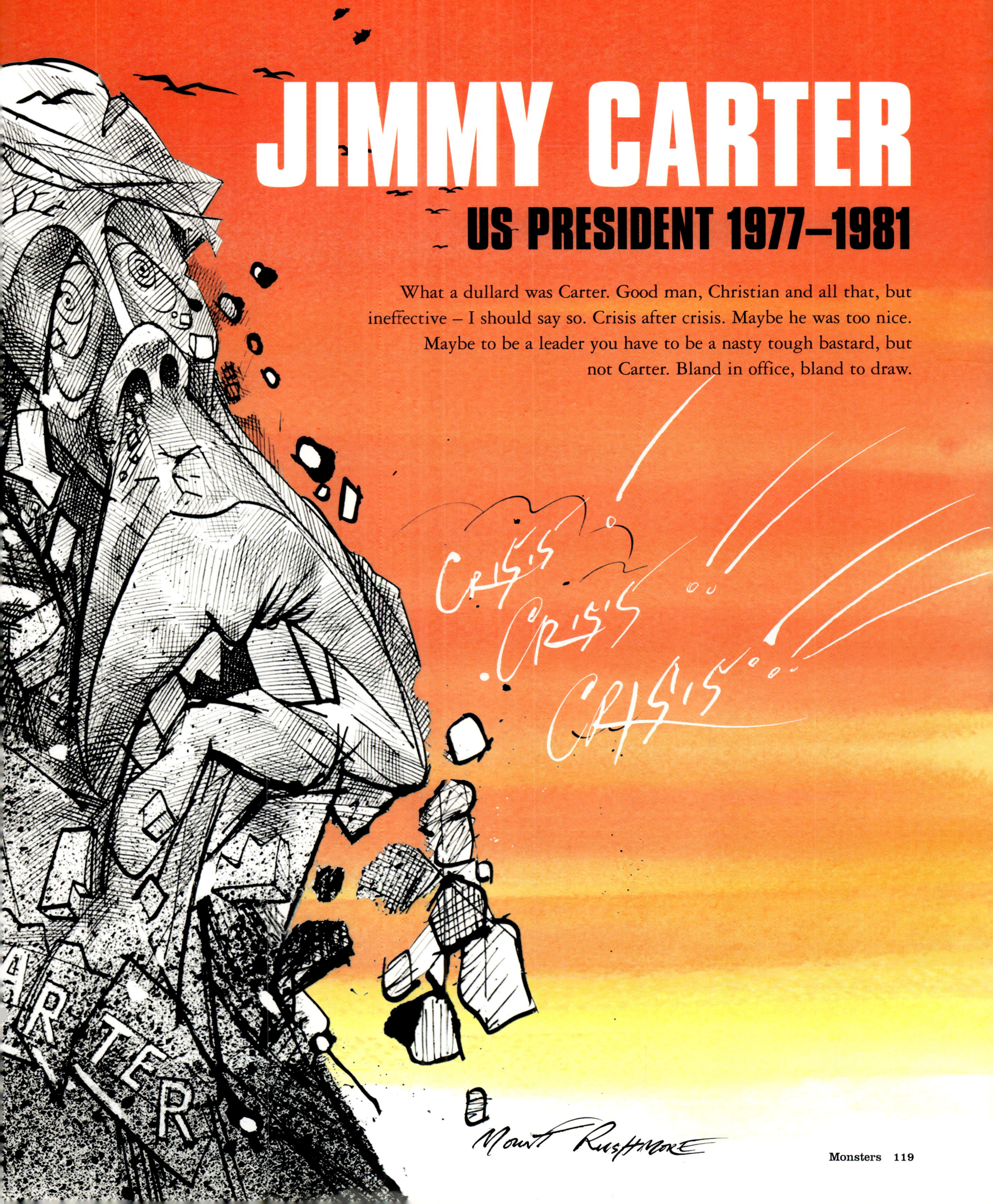

THE GREAT DEBATE ZZZZZZZZZZZZZ

I HAVE LUSTED AFTER POWER BUT PURELY A BIBLICAL SENSE

YES

A RICHER AND BETTER PLACE TO LIVE

WASHINGTON

WHAT THIS COUNTRY NEEDS IS

BLAH

PLAYBOY

WATERGATE

EXPENDITURE

AMNESTY

NIXON

PEANUTS

BALANCED BUDGET

YOU MAY THINK I LOOK STUPID BUT I CAN YOU

I WOULD LIKE TO SAY AT THIS POINT. WHERE

AND IN CONCLUSION

Contest to find the most powerful man in the world

Peanut Farmer

Carter the Peanut Farmer (his family owned a peanut business) was embarrassed by his beer-swilling brother Billy's connections with Libya.

Energy Crisis

Carter campaigned to save energy. He wanted to rein in the enormous wastage and thus make America less vulnerable to the dictates of Saudi Arabia and Iran.

(OPPOSITE) The great debate with Gerald Ford during presidential campaigning in 1976 – dull as dishwater. Enough people woke up and remembered to make their way to the polling stations for Carter to secure a narrow victory.

RUSSIA INVADES AFGHANISTAN

In December 1979, the Soviet Union invaded Afghanistan. With the 1980 election fast approaching, Carter was in a bind. Senator Edward Muskie appeals to Soviet Foreign Minister Andrei Gromyko while Republican front-runner Ronald Reagan hovers.

LET HIM GO GROMYKO OR WE'LL ALL HAVE REAGAN TO DEAL WITH

AFGHANISTAN

Carter invited President Anwar Sadat of Egypt and Prime Minister Menachem Begin of Israel to meet at Camp David for peace talks in September 1978. After initial hostility, Sadat and Begin were persuaded to negotiate. The two leaders won the Nobel Peace Prize later that year, and Carter's stock rose.

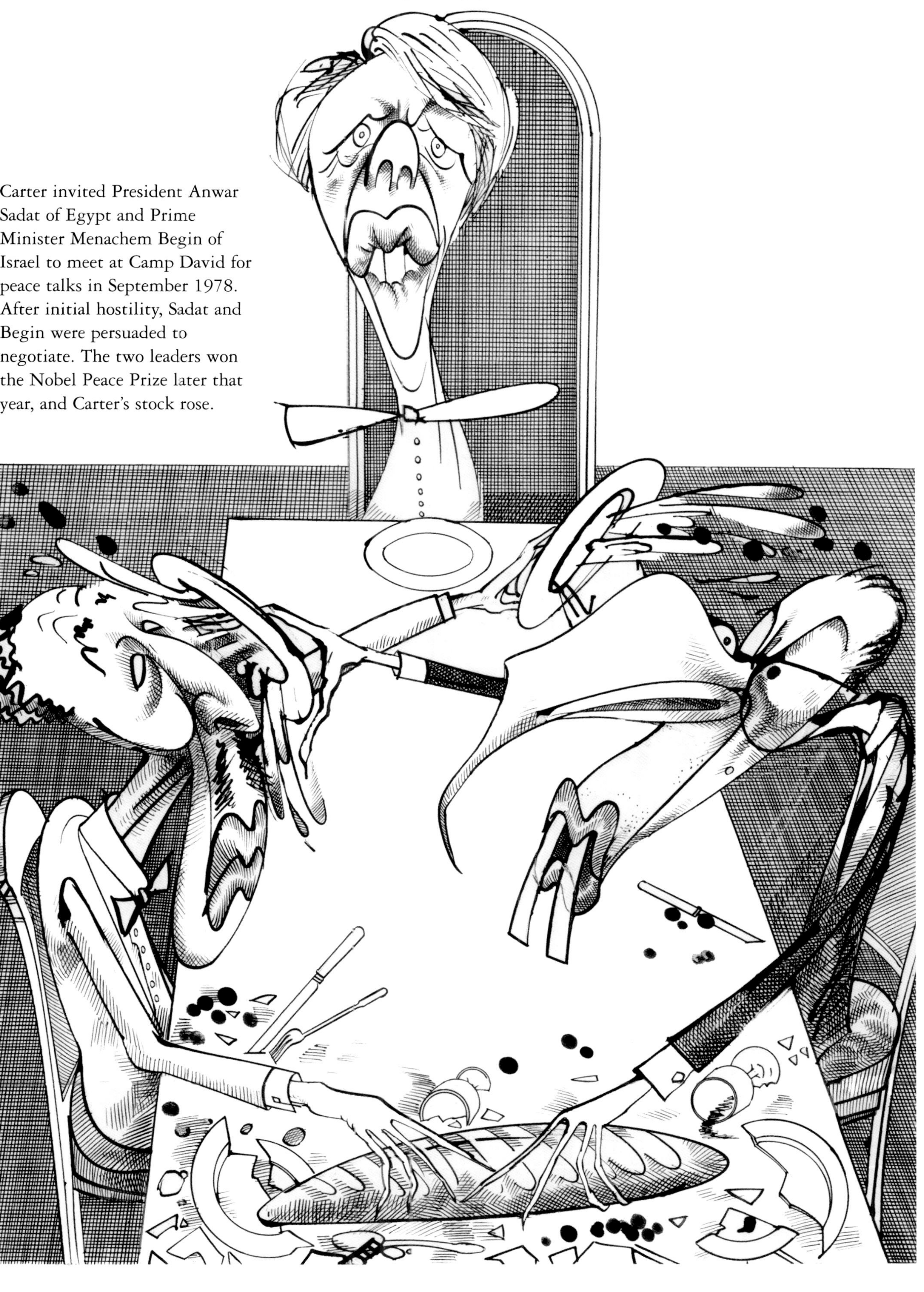

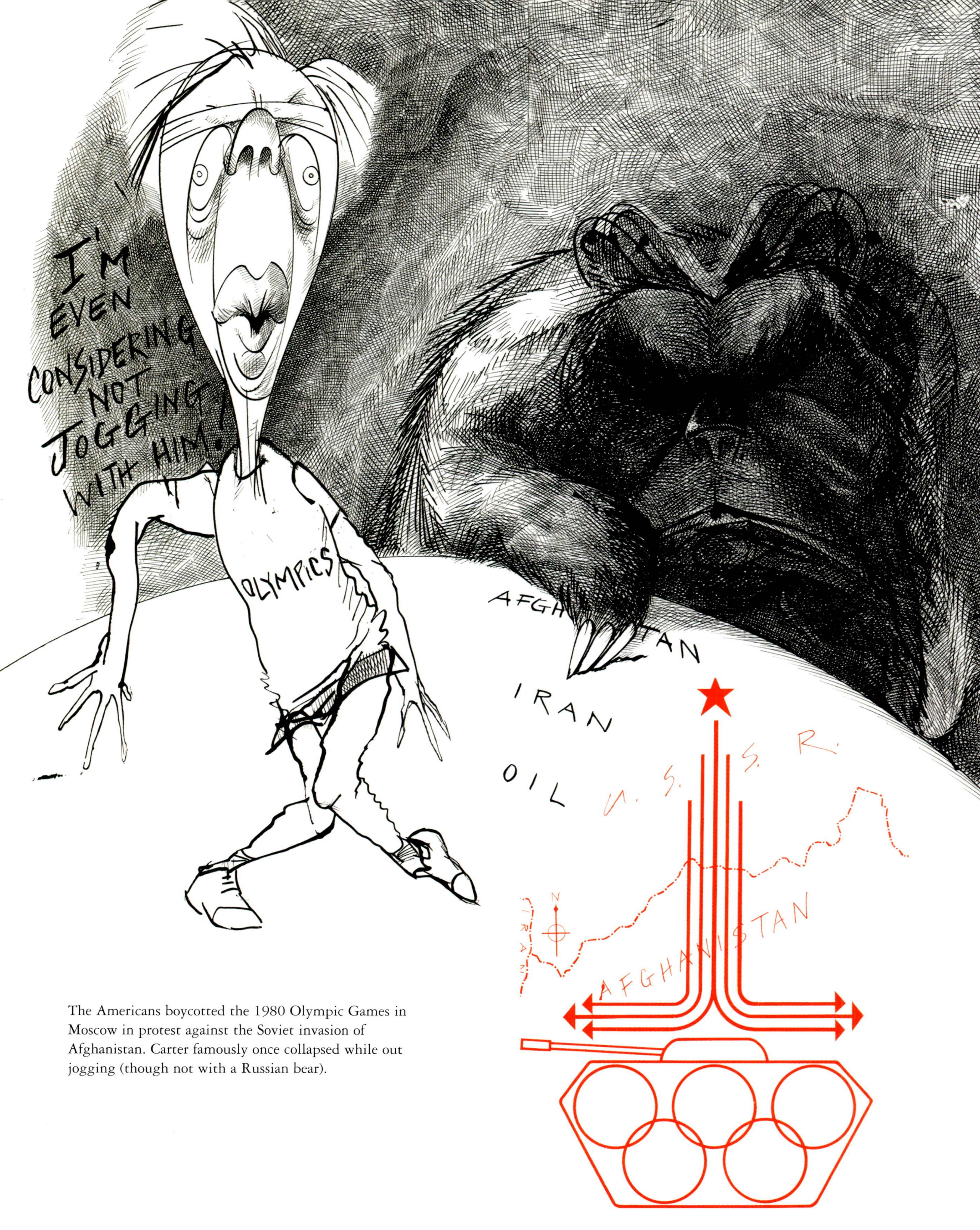

The Americans boycotted the 1980 Olympic Games in Moscow in protest against the Soviet invasion of Afghanistan. Carter famously once collapsed while out jogging (though not with a Russian bear).

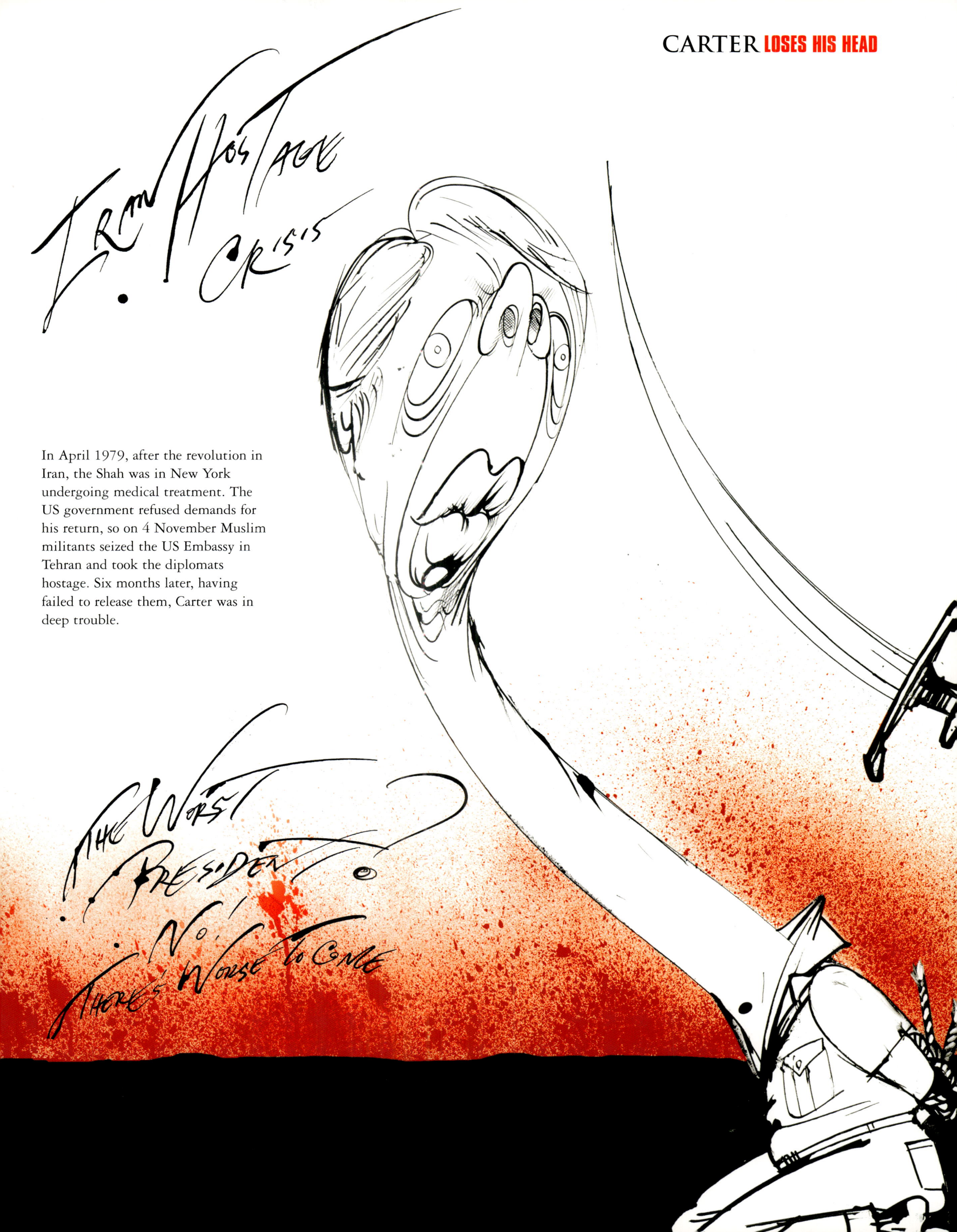

In April 1979, after the revolution in Iran, the Shah was in New York undergoing medical treatment. The US government refused demands for his return, so on 4 November Muslim militants seized the US Embassy in Tehran and took the diplomats hostage. Six months later, having failed to release them, Carter was in deep trouble.

INTERNATIONAL POLITICS

(LEFT) European premiers and finance ministers.

RUSSIA

A Brezhnev tank, and nuclear power – man's best friend.

(LEFT AND TOP SPREAD) The Balkans war of the early 1990s. Croatia was one of the first nations to break away from the Yugoslav Federation, leading to conflict with Serbia.

(BELOW) Yuri Andropov, the Soviet leader who died in office in 1984 just over a year after succeeding Brezhnev.

(OPPOSITE, RIGHT) Old habits die hard.

(OPPOSITE, FAR RIGHT) In the late 1980s, Lithuania was one of the Baltic republics agitating for independence.

EASTERN EUROPE

GLASNOST
COMMUNIST PARTY
THE NEW DEMOCRACY
ROMANIA
GRRRRRRRRR
INDEPENDENCE
LITHUANIA

CHINA

OPPOSITE

(TOP LEFT) In February 1973, Israel, represented here by Defence Minister General Moshe Dayan, shot down a Libyan airliner with the loss of 106 lives after it strayed into their airspace.

(MIDDLE LEFT) President Nasser of Egypt and General Dayan.

(LEFT) Unable to bring down Israel, Arab guerrillas threaten the stability of every Arab regime (December 1969).

THIS PAGE

(TOP) In the summer of 1978, with Lebanon torn by conflict, the Israelis prevented the Syrians from storming Christian-held east Beirut. Israeli leader Menachem Begin is the tank.

(ABOVE) By September 1981 Egyptian president Anwar Sadat's high hopes of peace with Israel had begun to founder and crack. He was assassinated by Muslim extremists the following month.

(RIGHT) Ariel Sharon uproots the West Bank inhabitants

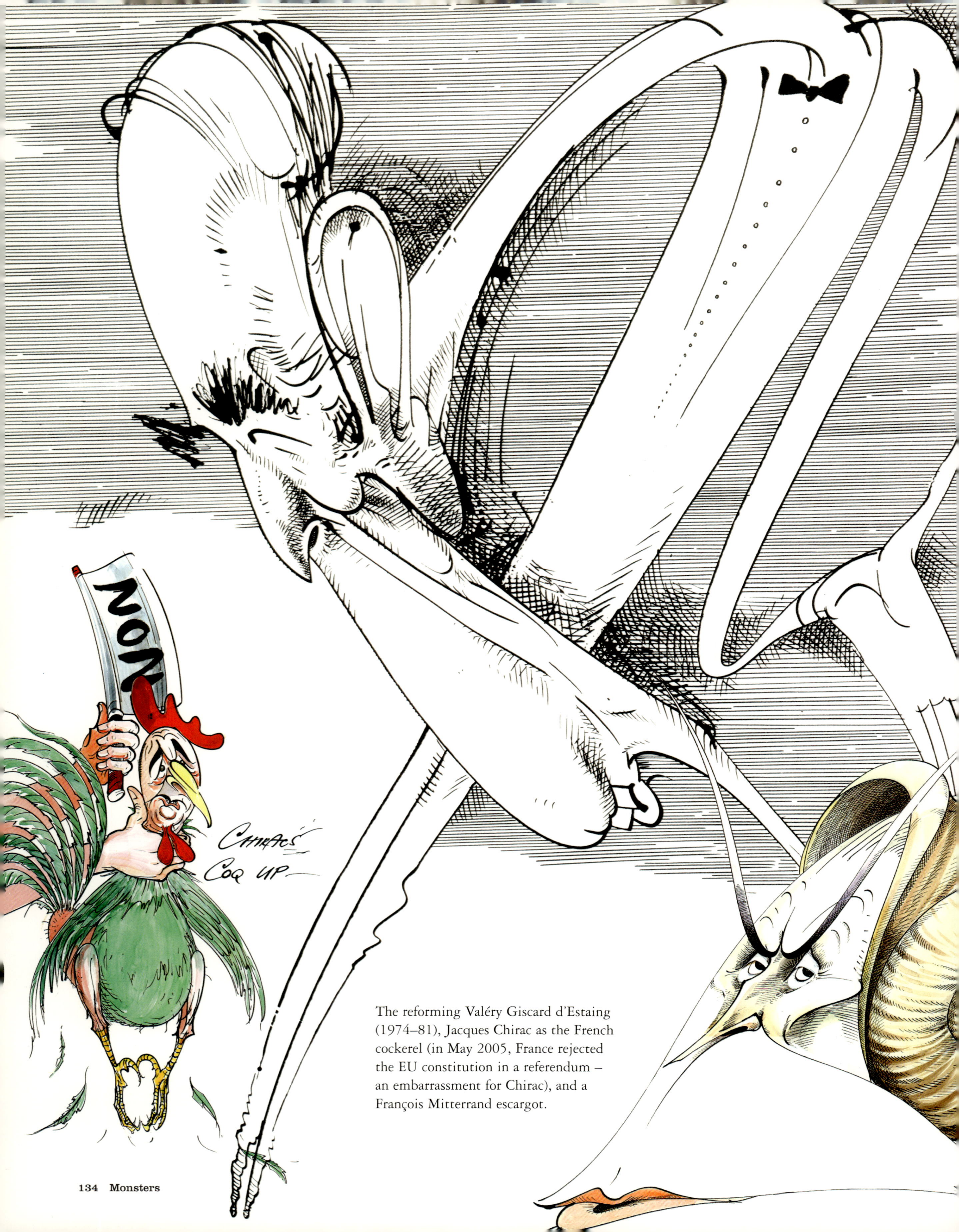

The reforming Valéry Giscard d'Estaing (1974–81), Jacques Chirac as the French cockerel (in May 2005, France rejected the EU constitution in a referendum – an embarrassment for Chirac), and a François Mitterrand escargot.

FRANCE

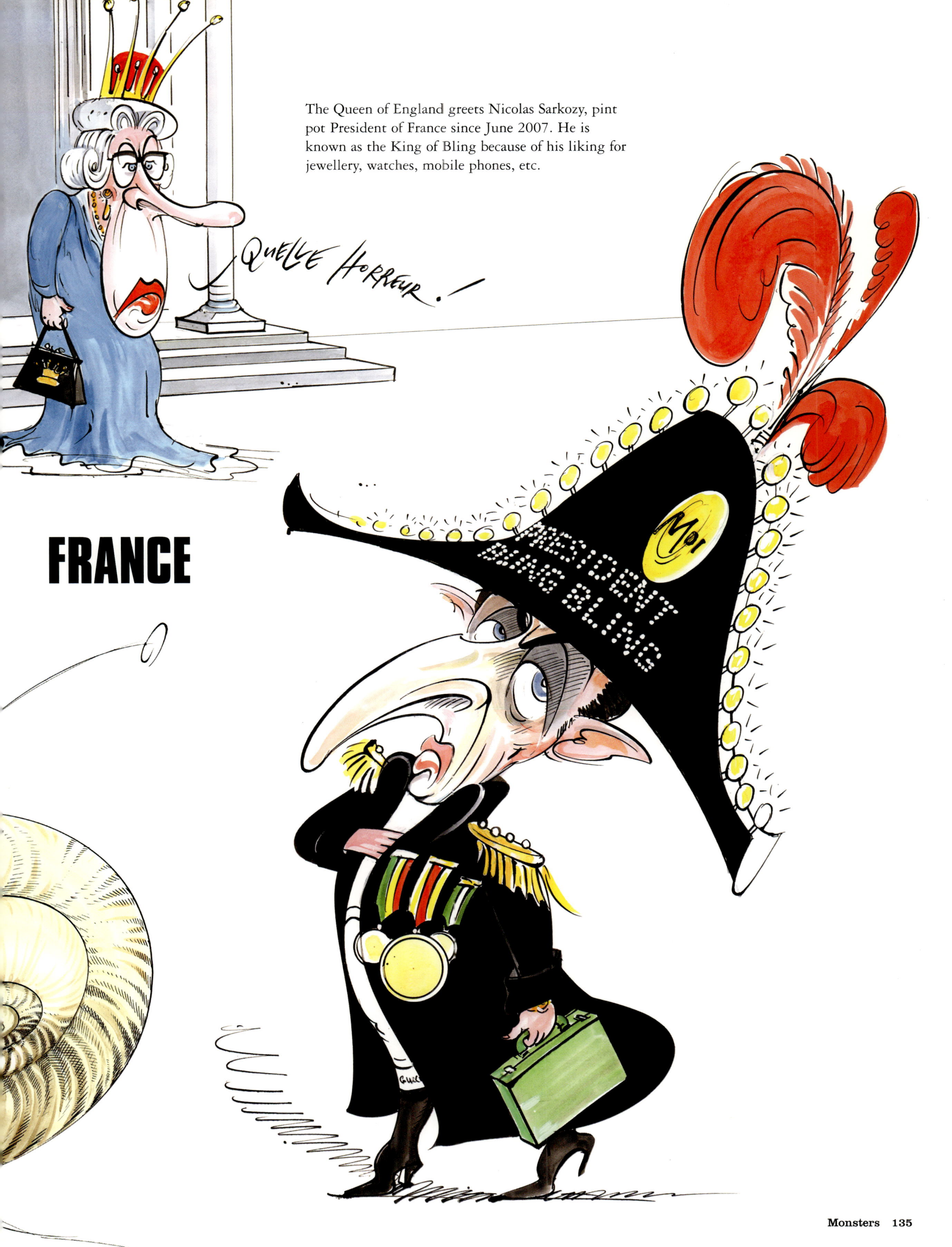

The Queen of England greets Nicolas Sarkozy, pint pot President of France since June 2007. He is known as the King of Bling because of his liking for jewellery, watches, mobile phones, etc.

GERMANY

(LEFT) Helmut Kohl as the Pied Piper of the Bundesbank.

(ABOVE) Helmut Schmidt, Chancellor from 1974, whose stated aim was 'the political unification of Europe in partnership with the US'.

(ABOVE RIGHT) Kohl again . . .

(RIGHT) The grand old statesman Konrad Adenauer, first Chancellor of the Federal Republic of Germany.

Now you're talking! I couldn't stand Mrs T, but she was wonderful to draw.

We always feel strongest about villains. From the first moment of her sickening speech quoting St Francis of Assisi in that carefully modulated tone when she won the election, she set me off. Did she really think all that waffle impressed? Are we that naive? Probably yes.

She had no discernible sense of humour and was completely unsympathetic to those who were not as strong as she. The only time we ever saw her cry was when she was forced out of office – sorry for herself, but not for others.

I always gave her a stabbing, aquiline nose, drooping eyes and a small mouth, full of bloody incisors. I could depict her as anything cutting, stabbing, slicing, biting, aggressive – like a dagger, a knife, an axe or scissors. Great material. She wouldn't have appreciated these drawings.

MARGARET THATCHER

PRIME MONSTER 1979–1990

THATCHER **MILK SNATCHER**

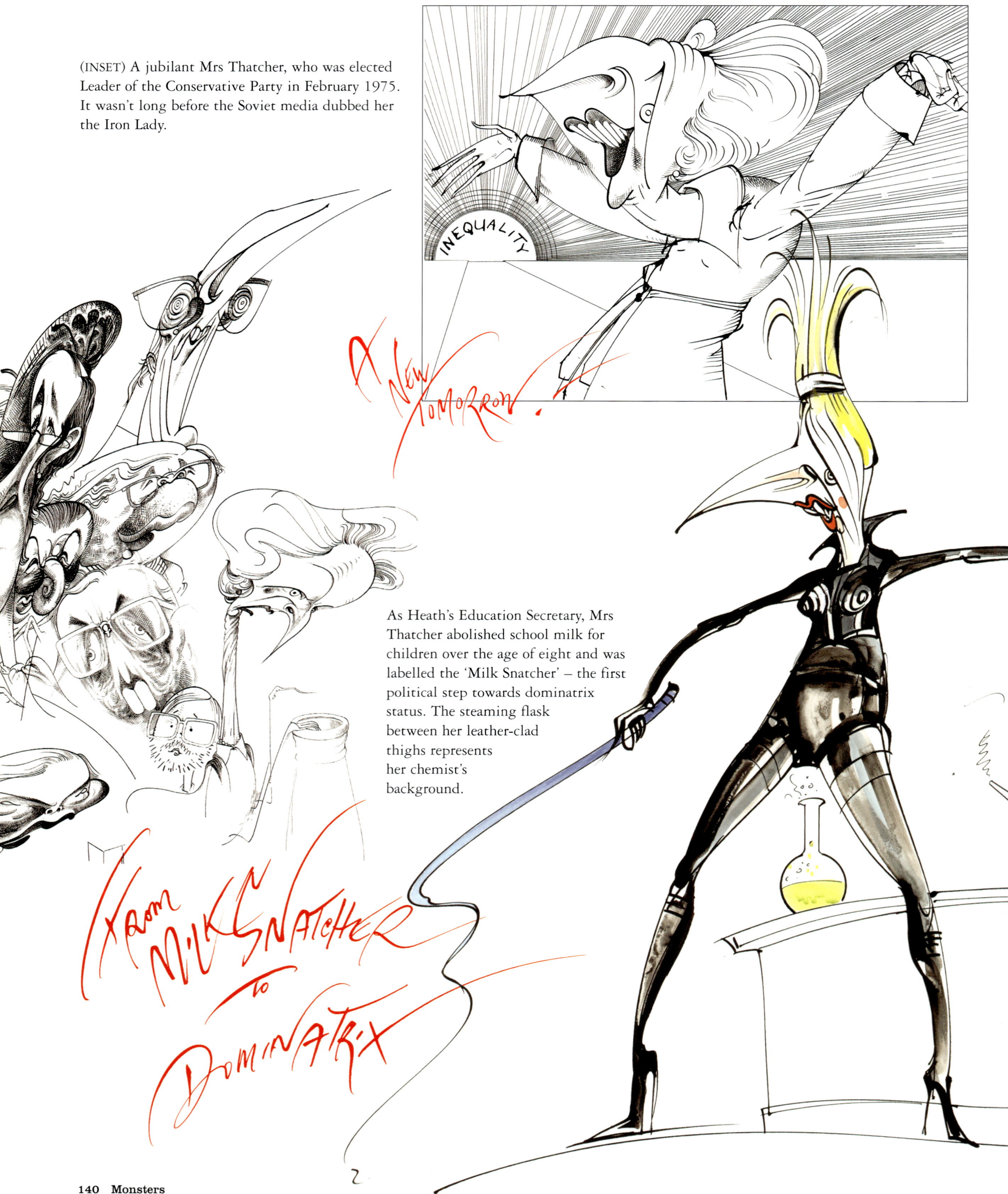

(INSET) A jubilant Mrs Thatcher, who was elected Leader of the Conservative Party in February 1975. It wasn't long before the Soviet media dubbed her the Iron Lady.

As Heath's Education Secretary, Mrs Thatcher abolished school milk for children over the age of eight and was labelled the 'Milk Snatcher' – the first political step towards dominatrix status. The steaming flask between her leather-clad thighs represents her chemist's background.

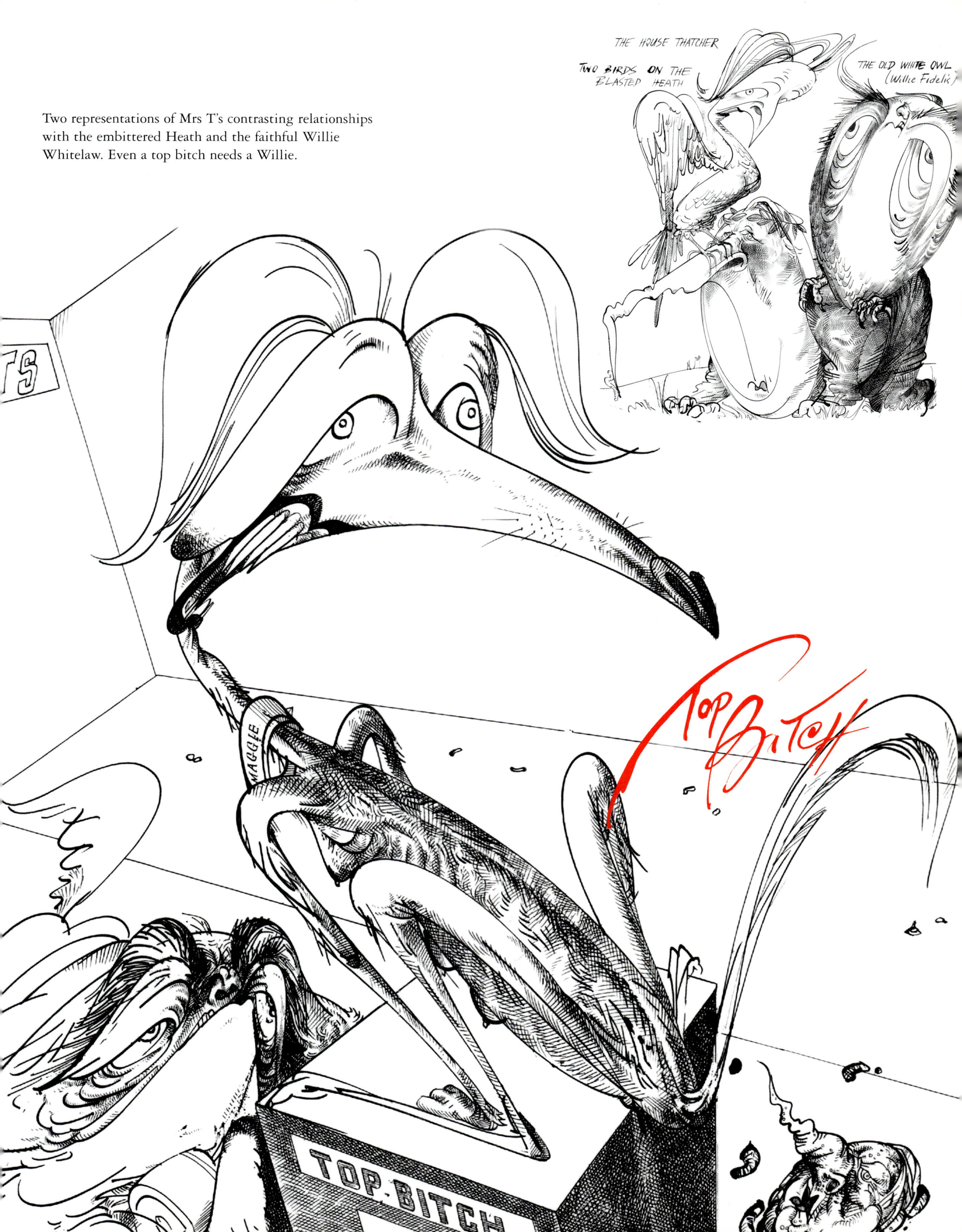

Two representations of Mrs T's contrasting relationships with the embittered Heath and the faithful Willie Whitelaw. Even a top bitch needs a Willie.

The versatility of Mrs T. I could transmogrify her into a shark, a bird of prey, an automaton, a Torydactyl, the Iron Lady, of course, an old bag and a mad cow.

THE IRON LADY

(BELOW) Tory policy and research supremo Keith Joseph. In a landmark lecture in 1976 he advocated monetarism, substantial cuts in tax and public spending, and incentives for wealth creators – the pillars of Thatcherism.

(OPPOSITE, TOP) Mrs Thatcher becomes the new leader of the Conservative party and picks her Shadow Cabinet. In come Reginald Maudling and Lord Hailsham, out go Peter Walker, Robert Carr and Geoffrey Rippen.

(BELOW, left to right) Thatcher, Willie Whitelaw, Francis Pym, Geoffrey Howe, Jim Prior, Alec Douglas-Home and a disconsolate Ted Heath . . . the race for the leadership of the Conservative Party in 1975 – all the dignity of a primary-school pancake race. It was thought that Whitelaw would win. Thatcher was said to have a quick but suburban mind.

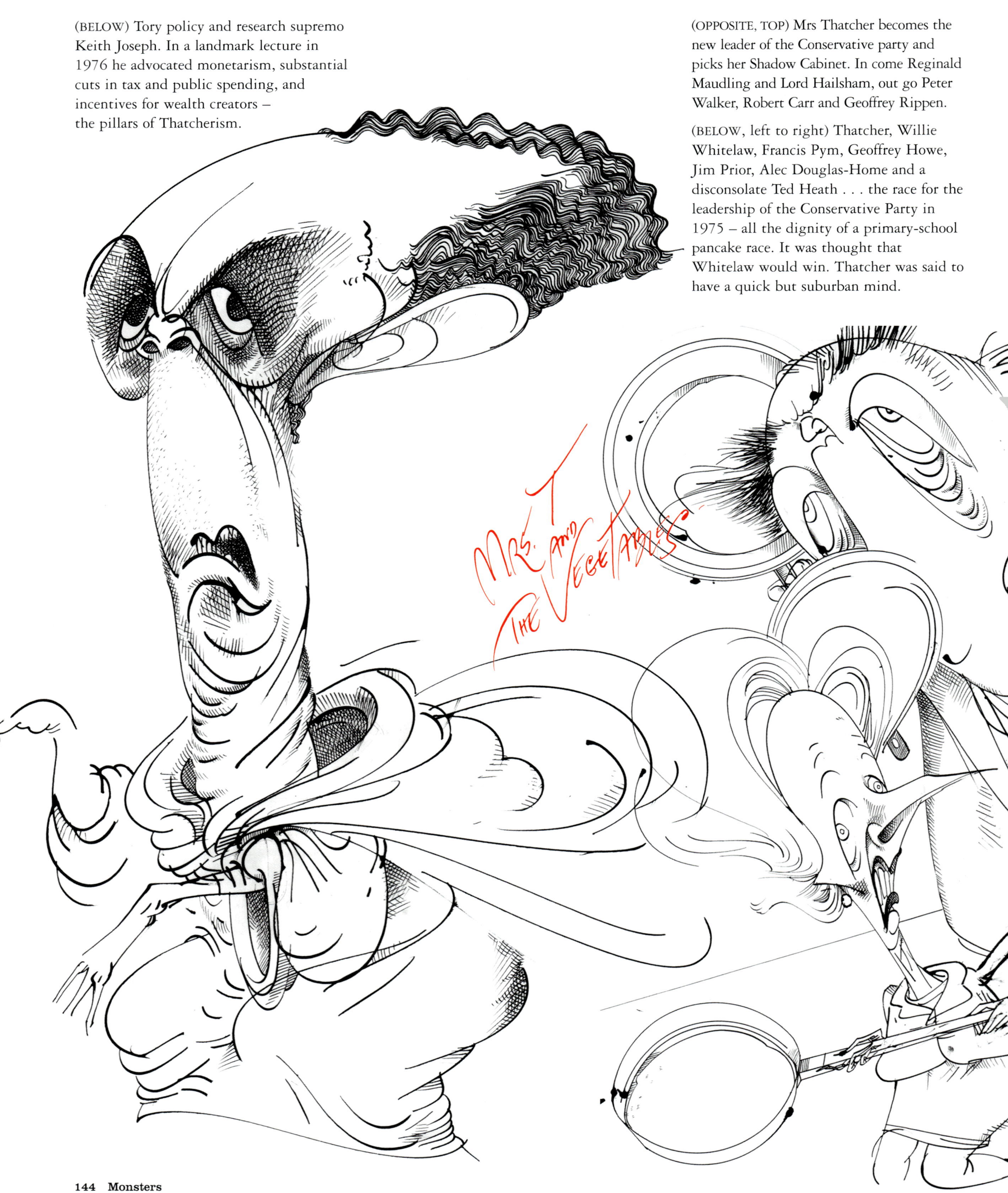

OLD MOTHER THATCHER
WENT TO HER CABINET
TO GIVE HER POOR PARTY SOME BONE
WHEN THE HOARDER GOTTHERE
THE TALENT WAS BARE
SO SHE DUG UP
OLD MAUDLING AND CO.
WHERE AM I?
SACKED
OUT
THE BOOT
RULES

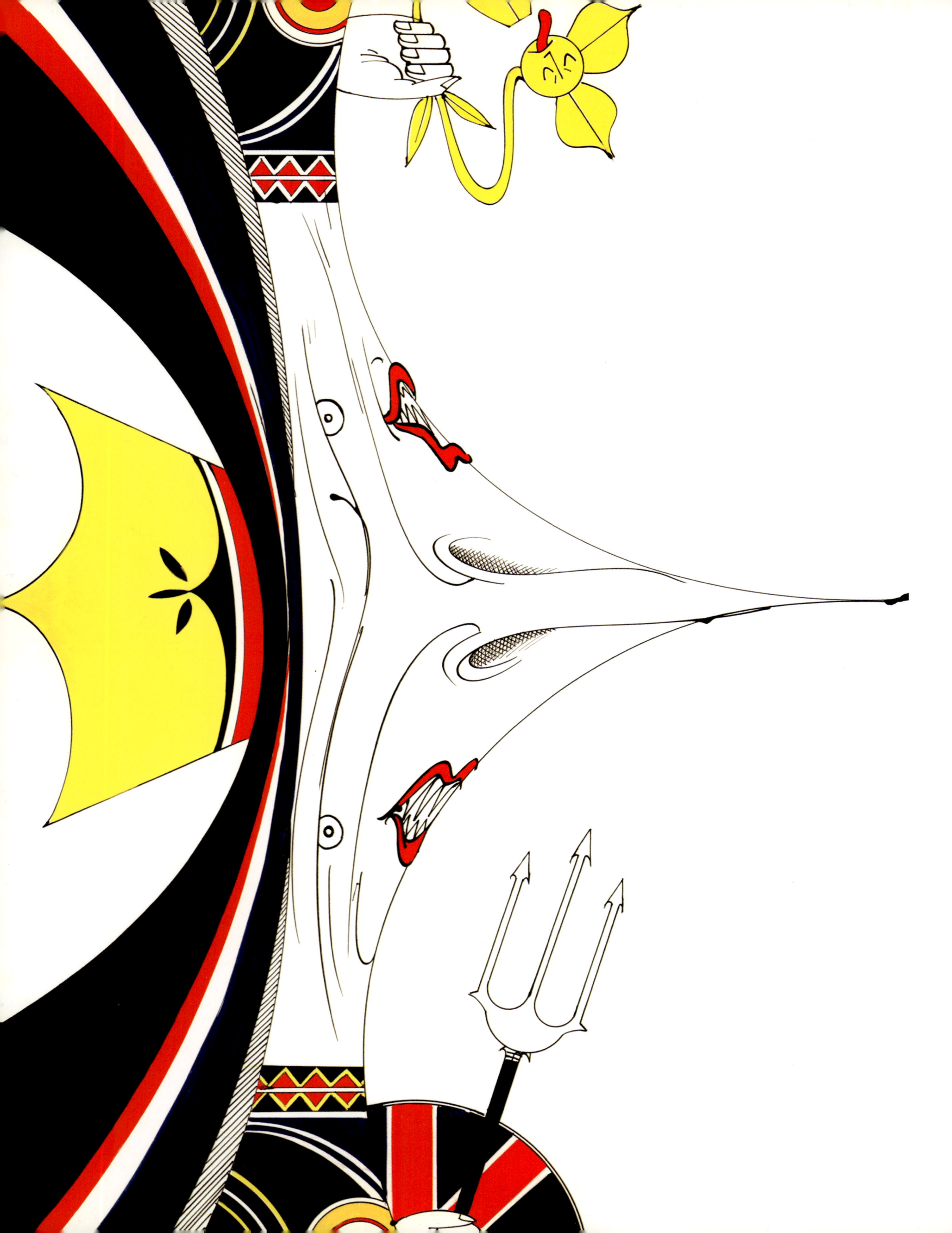

Margaret Thatcher as the Queen of Hearts and (from top to bottom) three of her knaves: Geoffrey Howe, Willie Whitelaw and Francis Pym.

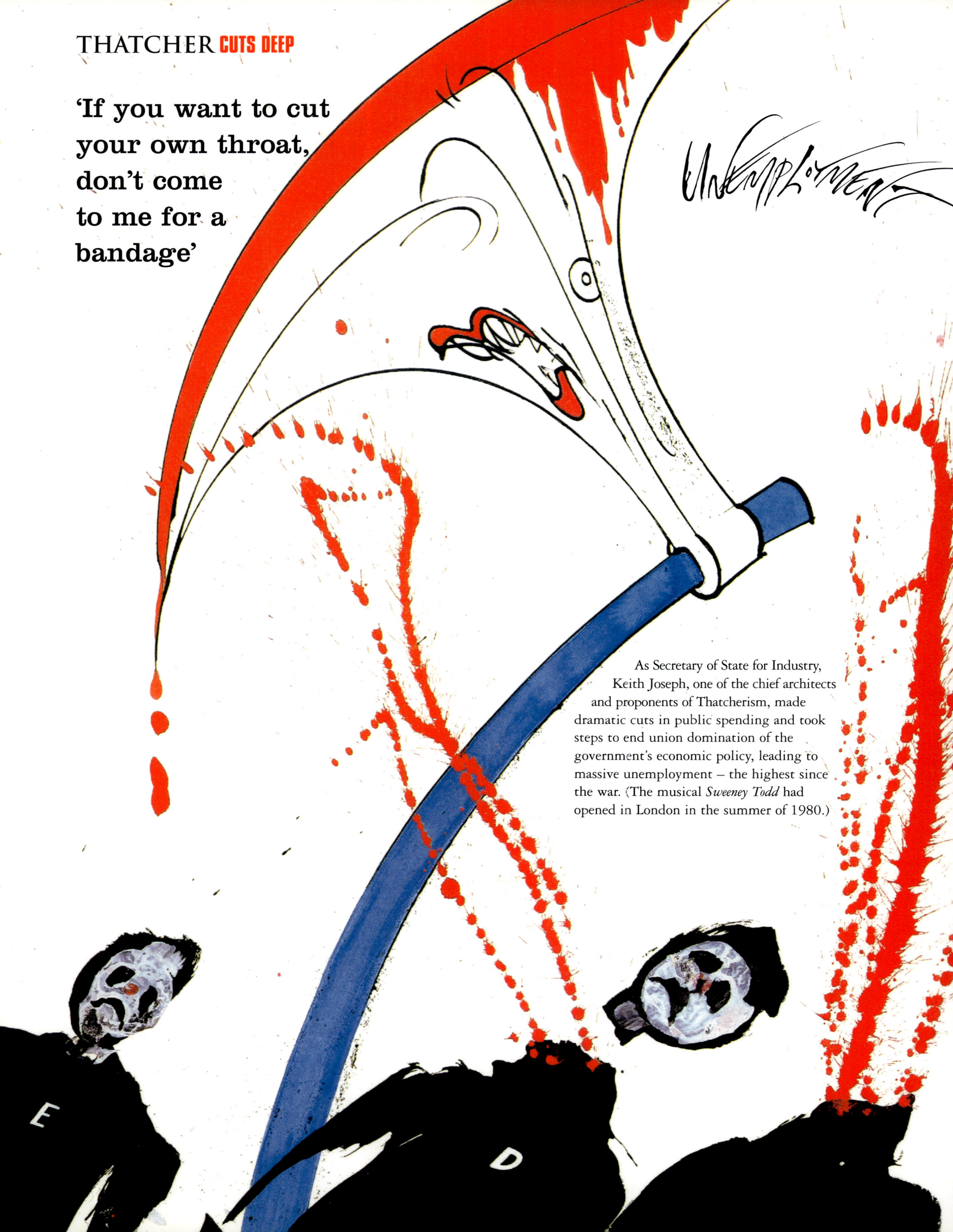

'If you want to cut your own throat, don't come to me for a bandage'

As Secretary of State for Industry, Keith Joseph, one of the chief architects and proponents of Thatcherism, made dramatic cuts in public spending and took steps to end union domination of the government's economic policy, leading to massive unemployment – the highest since the war. (The musical *Sweeney Todd* had opened in London in the summer of 1980.)

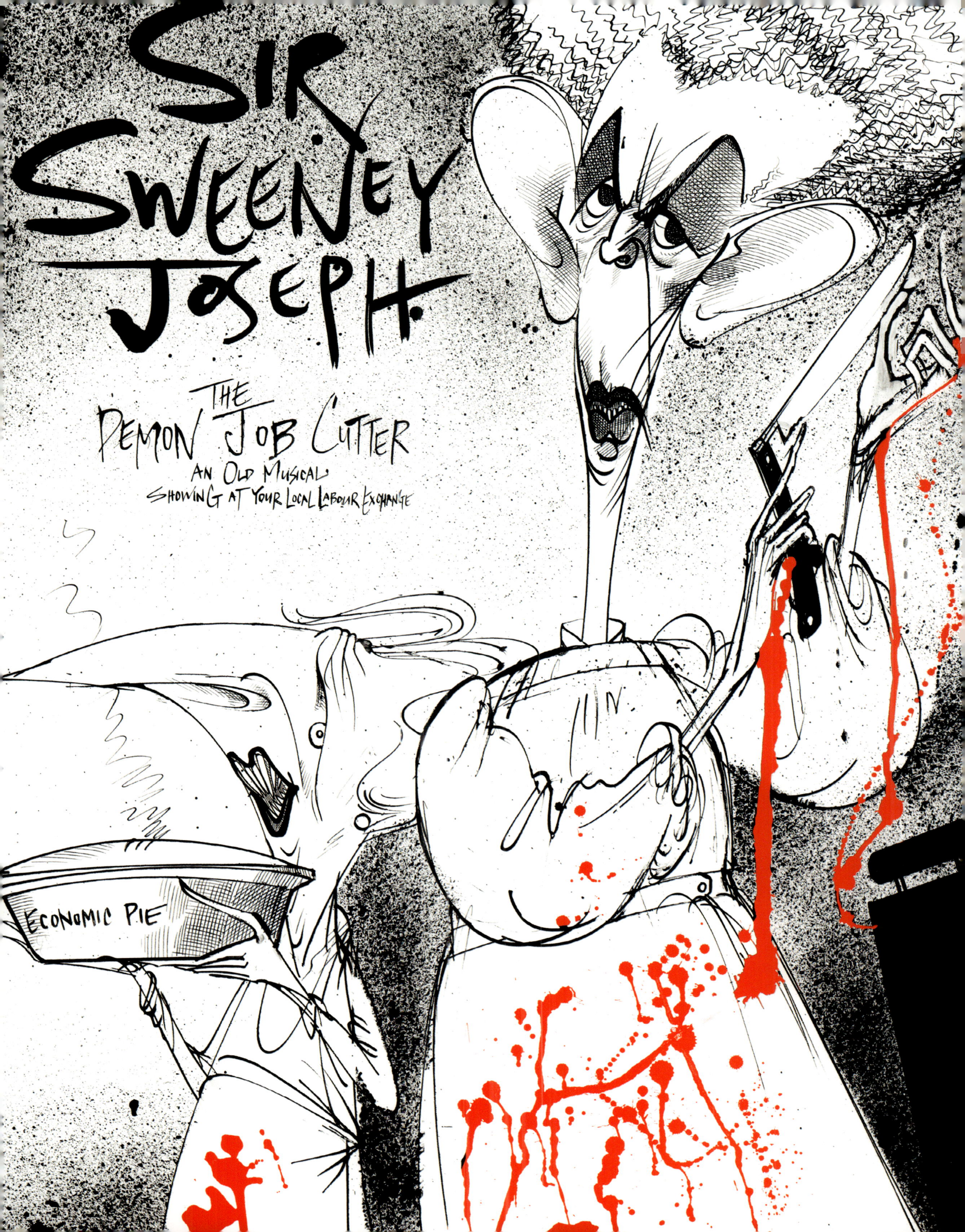
SIR SWEENEY JOSEPH
THE DEMON JOB CUTTER
AN OLD MUSICAL
SHOWING AT YOUR LOCAL LABOUR EXCHANGE
ECONOMIC PIE

Queen and Country
MAGGIE V
ONCE MORE UNTO THE BREACH
DEAR FRIENDS ONCE MORE
OR CLOSE THE WALL UP WITH
OUR ENGLISH UNEMPLOYED
THEN A SOLDIER
FULL OF STRANGE OATHS,
WOULD YOU MIND
YOUR MAJESTY –
RULING FOREVER?
– OH, VERY WELL.

(OPPOSITE) A crusading Margaret Thatcher as Shakespeare's Henry V before the walls of Harfleur, and in more queenly mode.

(RIGHT) Mrs T quickly gained a reputation for being a lady with *cojones*, principally, in the early 1980s, as a result of her dismissive attitude towards the so-called 'wets' in her Cabinet, Jim Prior and Francis Pym among them.

The face that launched the Task Force. In April 1982, under General Galtieri, Argentina invaded and seized control of the British-administered Falkland Islands – known as the Malvinas to the Argentinians, who had always considered them part of their country. Mrs Thatcher ordered a task force to set sail, which by June had retaken the islands. Mrs T was overjoyed and the Falklands victory helped to ensure a landslide in the following year's election despite increasing troubles at home, not the least of them who would pay for the war. The cost of maintaining the Falklands alone was estimated at 100 million pounds.

THE
FALKLANDS
1982
NEW
FOLLY
PROPOSED
ON THIS
SITE
£100 MILLION
HMS INVINCIBLE

S.O.S.
H.M.S. DESPAIR
LEON BRITT
MARGARET THATC
CONSERVATIVE PARTY
REMAINS OF POUND FOUND
DR. THATCHERSTEIN TO REMODEL MONHSTER
N.H.S
NUPE
COHSE
HOSPITAL
CLOSED
STRIKE
ER! SCALPEL! FORCEPS.. HOSPITAL HOTEL CHARGES.. PRIVATE HEALTH SCHEME! TAX CONCESSIONS PRIVATE INVESTMENT IN HEALTH SERVICE ETC.!

(LEFT) In May 1985, Thatcher and David Owen fought it out in the county elections. The SDP–Liberal Alliance was poised for a breakthrough, and the Conservatives lost in county halls across the country, having failed to reduce unemployment.

(OPPOSITE PAGE)

(TOP LEFT) In October 1989, after over six years as Chancellor, Nigel Lawson dramatically resigned – the first act of Mrs T's downfall. His firmly leashed replacement, John Major, busily bails out.

(BOTTOM LEFT) Lawson with Tory chairman Kenneth Baker just a few weeks earlier, unearthing a declining pound.

(TOP RIGHT) Trade and Industry Secretary Leon Brittan crumbles and resigns during the Westland affair in 1986.

(BOTTOM RIGHT) Dr Thatcherstein begins an operation on the ungainly NHS.

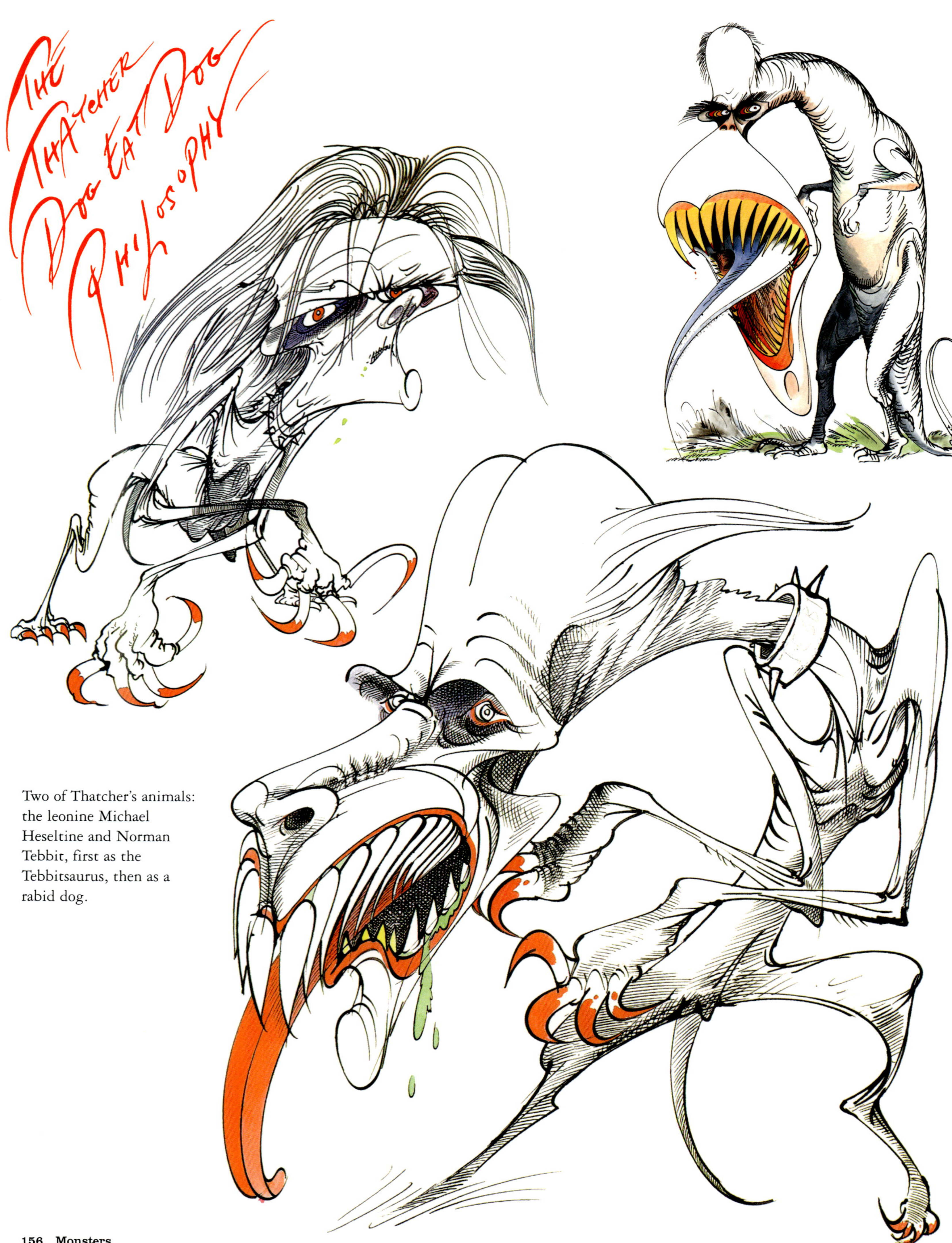

Two of Thatcher's animals: the leonine Michael Heseltine and Norman Tebbit, first as the Tebbitsaurus, then as a rabid dog.

(ABOVE) Mother Kissmass with the Icy Heart Walks the Frozen Wastes.

(ABOVE RIGHT) Nanny Thatcher nurses a mewling, puking Norman Tebbit.

(RIGHT) Get Thee Hence. In the autumn of 1983, Cecil Parkinson's secretary Sara Keays disclosed that she was carrying his baby. Despite being a close confidant of the PM, Mrs Thatcher dismissed her party chairman from the Cabinet.

REBELLION AND DOWNFALL

(RIGHT) Defence Secretary Michael Heseltine, the armaments salesman.

(BELOW) November 1990. Heseltine challenged Mrs Thatcher for the leadership of the Conservative Party when mad cow disease was rife and was said to be spreading to cats. The rallying call was the resignation speech of Mrs T's longest-serving minister, Geoffrey Howe. Denis Healey may once have likened facing Howe to 'being savaged by a dead sheep', but he did for Mrs T with some stinging criticism, accusing her in cricketing analogy of being the team captain who broke the bats of her players before they went out to the crease.

(MAIN PICTURE) Mrs Thatcher nears the end, besieged and attacked on all sides.

(TOP RIGHT) In 1990, Mrs Thatcher was hell bent on introducing the community charge, or 'poll tax' as it was popularly known, despite massive opposition to this levy on individuals regardless of means.

DON'T FORGET I WAS THE ARCHITECT OF ALL THIS...
NOT JOHN MAJOR!
POLL TAX FIASCO
REPOSSESSIONS
BANKRUPTCIES
UNEMPLOYMENT
ETC.
ETC.
ETC.
FOR SALE

A discarded and deranged Mrs Thatcher reminds an ungrateful country of her achievements.

(RIGHT) My take on the Britain Mrs Thatcher created.

The Ghosts of Belgrano

AS SHE WAS HAUNTED
SO SHE HAUNTED
THOSE THAT
FOLLOWED HER

A statement on Mrs Thatcher's peculiar matriarchal relationship with her successors John Major and William Hague.

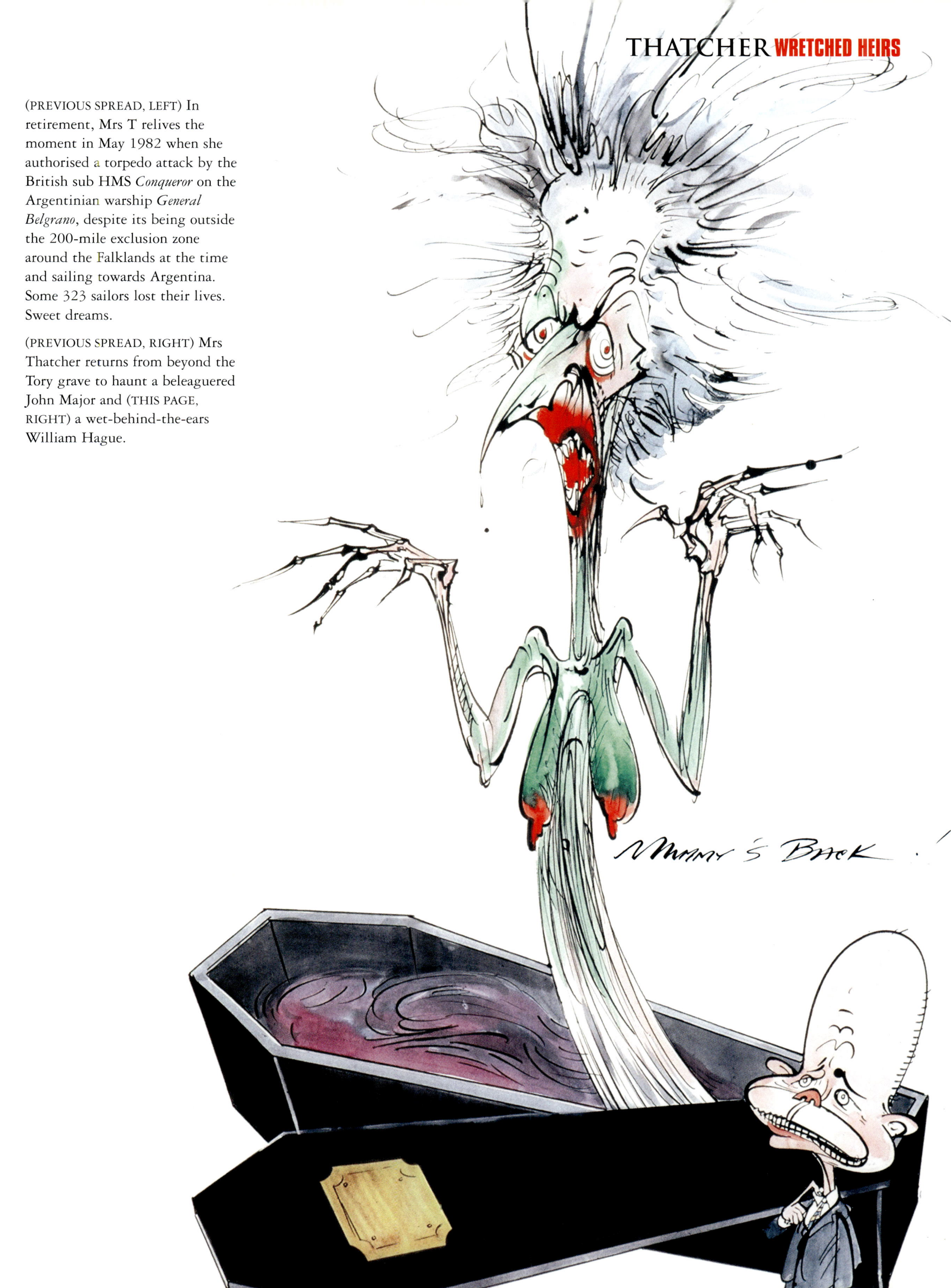

(PREVIOUS SPREAD, LEFT) In retirement, Mrs T relives the moment in May 1982 when she authorised a torpedo attack by the British sub HMS *Conqueror* on the Argentinian warship *General Belgrano*, despite its being outside the 200-mile exclusion zone around the Falklands at the time and sailing towards Argentina. Some 323 sailors lost their lives. Sweet dreams.

(PREVIOUS SPREAD, RIGHT) Mrs Thatcher returns from beyond the Tory grave to haunt a beleaguered John Major and (THIS PAGE, RIGHT) a wet-behind-the-ears William Hague.

US PRESIDENT 1981–1989

RONALD REAGAN

I usually depicted Reagan as a Mickey Mouse figure because he was seen as a rather simplistic man and, of course, he had been a film star for a significant part of his career.

'You can tell a lot about a fellow's character by his way of eating jelly beans'

(TOP) When he first came to power, Reagan had a reputation for being a Republican warmonger. Who would have thought that he would be the American president who oversaw the end of the Cold War?

(BELOW) February 1981, and Secretary of State General Alexander Haig, cradling a neutron bomb, encourages the newly elected Reagan, who was talking tough at the time, calling the Soviets cheats and liars and accusing them of terrorism.

(OPPOSITE) Ronald Reagan and his running mate George Bush in July 1980, preparing for the election.

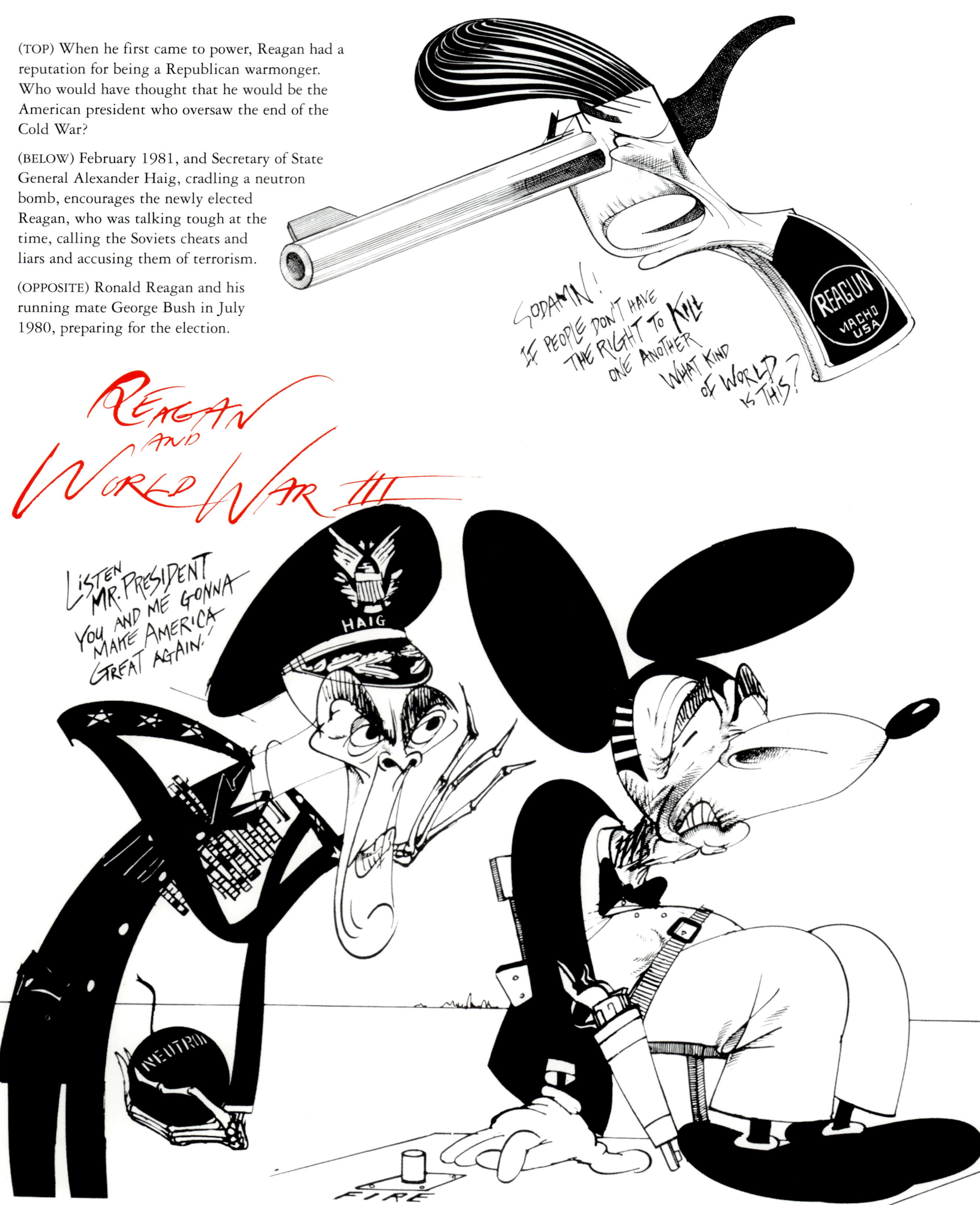

FORD
DARLING YOU WILL BE DREADFUL STOP
ON STAGE MR. REAGUN
SHOOTING REHEARSAL FOR WORLD WAR III
HAIR DYE
RE-JUVENAT-ION PILLS

(OPPOSITE TOP) Towards the end of 1986, Reagan came under strong criticism for his policy of secret gun-running to Iran, arms for hostages and illicit money-laundering. The President's men had diverted the proceeds from the sale of arms to Iran to fund the 'Contras' fighting the left-wing government in Nicaragua, despite the wish of Congress that no military aid should be sent.

(OPPOSITE BELOW) In April 1986, Libya was bombed as a 'self-defence' measure against terrorist attacks targeting US citizens. Here, Reagan and Colonel Gaddafi snarl at each other. Mrs Thatcher was seen as Reagan's poodle for allowing American bombers to fly from British bases – a canine tradition later embraced with enthusiasm by Tony Blair.

In his first term, Reagan was adversarial towards the USSR, vastly increasing the defence budget to a 100 billion dollars. Without consulting his allies, in 1981 he went ahead with the development of the neutron bomb, an alternative warhead for short-range weapons. There was a certain amount of anxiety around at the time about this former Hollywood star being the most powerful man in the world.

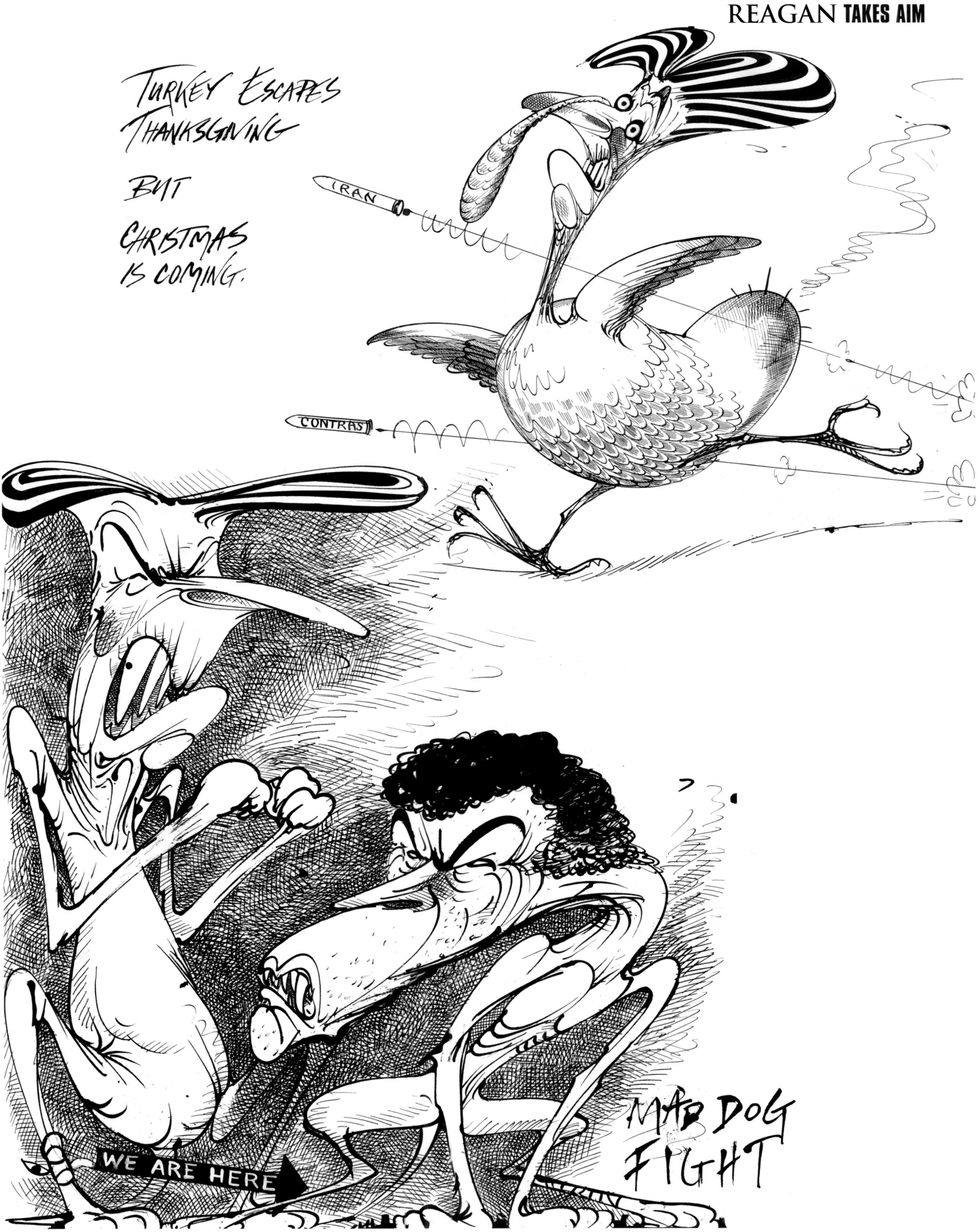
TURKEY ESCAPES THANKSGIVING
BUT
CHRISTMAS IS COMING.
IRAN
CONTRAS
WE ARE HERE
MAD DOG FIGHT

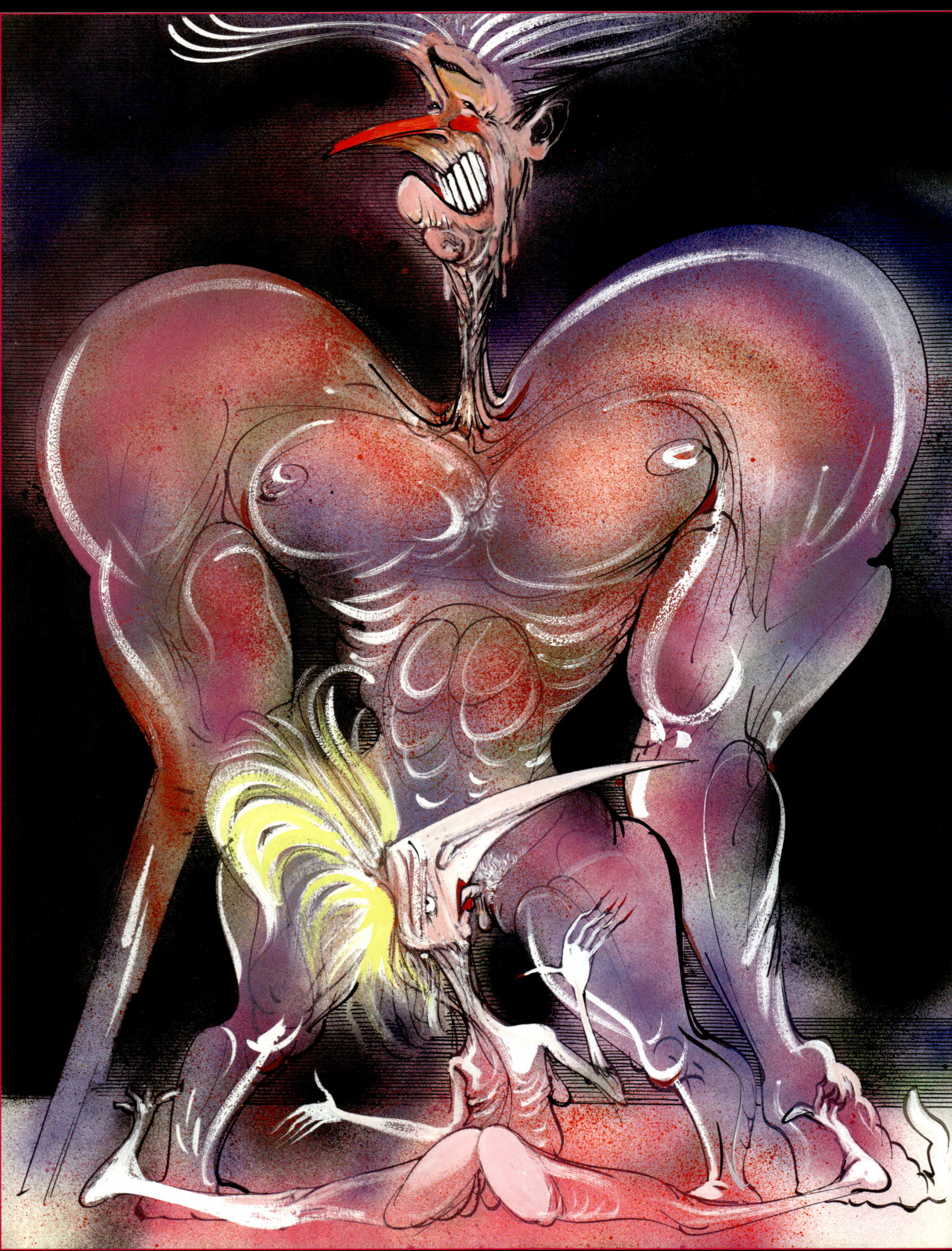

That old 'special relationship' again.

WELCOME MIKHAIL FROM RON
HEY! THIS IS MY BIG MOMENT
WELCOME MIKHAIL
NEW BLOOMS IN MOSCOW
KREMLIN CONSERVATISM
IF YOU GO OUT THERE HE MAY GET US BOTH
LITHUANIA
LATVIA

OPPOSITE

(TOP LEFT) Reagan set up a prestigious meeting with Gorbachev in Washington for December 1987, but Mrs Thatcher pipped him to the post by seeing the Soviet premier in England as he was en route. Gorbachev had already delivered his vision of the USSR's future in his book *Perestroika* ('Reconstruction'). He claimed that Soviet society was ripe for change, that there had been too many official lies.

(TOP RIGHT) Reagan the Peace Dove. In May 1988, he visited Gorbachev in Moscow. Human rights were discussed; the withdrawal of Soviet forces from Afghanistan continued; ratification documents of a treaty on intermediate and short-range missiles were signed. At the Communist Party Conference in Moscow, Gorbachev declared his intention to continue with his policy of liberalisation.

(BELOW) Gorby as Mother Russia warns her chickens of the dangers of leaving the country.

THIS PAGE

(RIGHT) Eventually, Gorbachev's reign came to a close and the new management was run by . . .

Boris Yeltsin, who got drunk and fell over a lot. Good fun to draw, but generally in a landscape position (BELOW).

Reagan's Decline
HELL NANCE,
ARE
YOU THE
PRESIDENT
OR AM I?
I CAN'T
REMEMBER

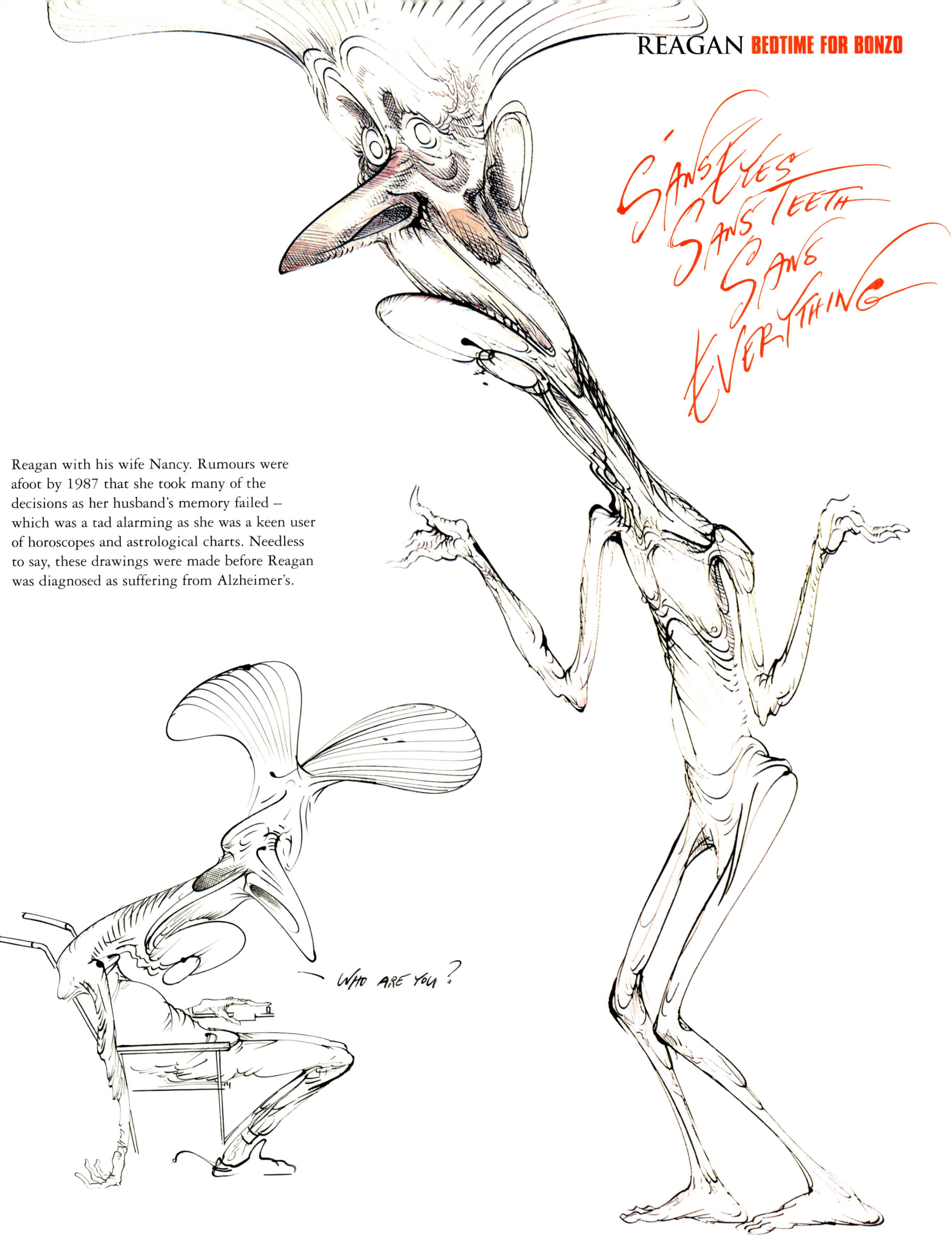

Reagan with his wife Nancy. Rumours were afoot by 1987 that she took many of the decisions as her husband's memory failed – which was a tad alarming as she was a keen user of horoscopes and astrological charts. Needless to say, these drawings were made before Reagan was diagnosed as suffering from Alzheimer's.

GEORGE BUSH

US PRESIDENT 1989–1993

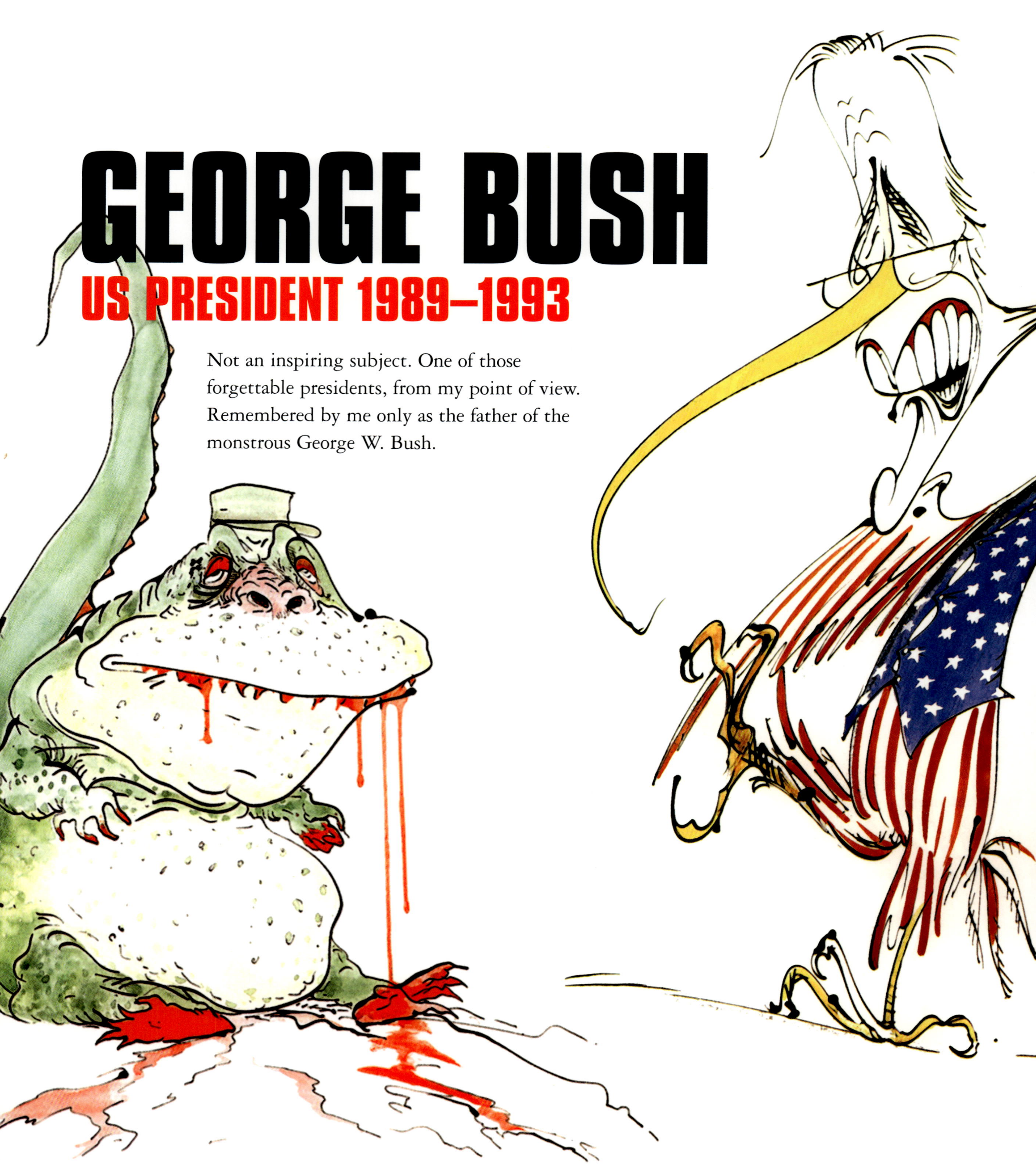

Not an inspiring subject. One of those forgettable presidents, from my point of view. Remembered by me only as the father of the monstrous George W. Bush.

READ MY LIPS!
I'M A LIAR
SO LONG GEORGE — YOU PICK UP THE TAB
THE BILL
PINEAPPLES CAN BITE!
MENU
NORIEGA

OPPOSITE

(LEFT) During his presidential campaign in 1988, Bush notoriously said that he would not raise taxes, adding 'read my lips' to emphasise the truth of the statement. He reneged on it later.

(TOP RIGHT) Reagan rides off into the sunset in January 1989, leaving Bush with an enormous deficit.

(BELOW RIGHT) Panama's General Manuel Noriega, formerly a close CIA and Washington ally, had by the end of 1989 become a prickly customer, accused by the US of drug-trafficking and other misdemeanours. In December, Bush initiated a military campaign to get rid of him.

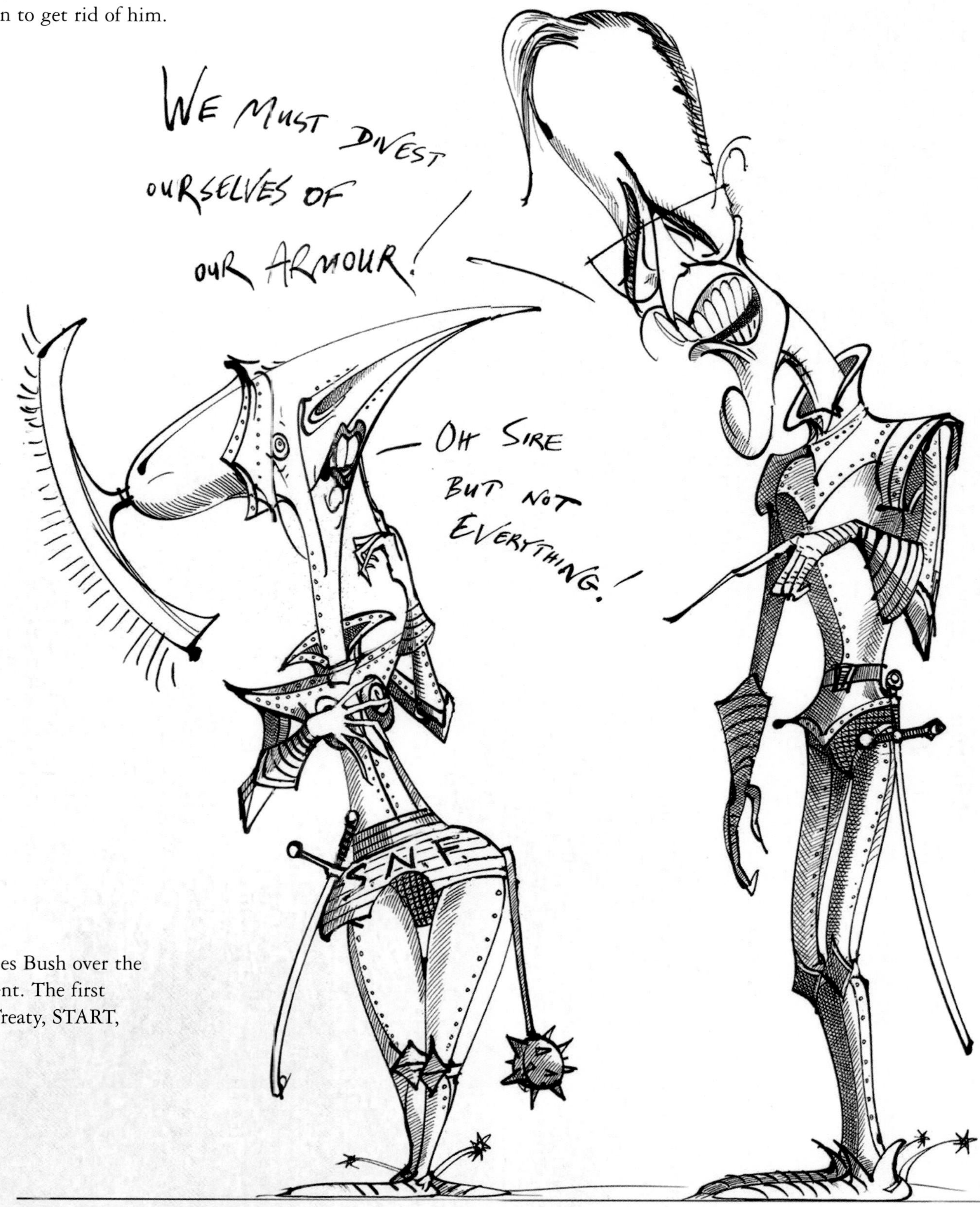

(RIGHT) Mrs Thatcher queries Bush over the extent of nuclear disarmament. The first Strategic Arms Reduction Treaty, START, was signed in 1991.

'When I need a little advice about Saddam Hussein, I turn to country music'

Saddam's invasion of Kuwait in August 1990. Initially (bottom left) Bush was confused as to what action to take because Saddam was a loose cannon in a geopolitically sensitive area of the world. He remained something of a tricky target even when coalition forces were unleashed, prepared as he was to use so-called 'human shields'.

(OPPOSITE) Bush appealed to Congress for more money and troops to tackle Saddam amid vocal domestic opposition to the war.

WHAT'S THAT DISTANT GUNFIRE?
GROWING U.S. DISSENT
PLEASE SEND 100,000 MORE TROOPS – AND ARMS, BOMBS ETC.
Yours
LETTER FROM THE TRENCHES

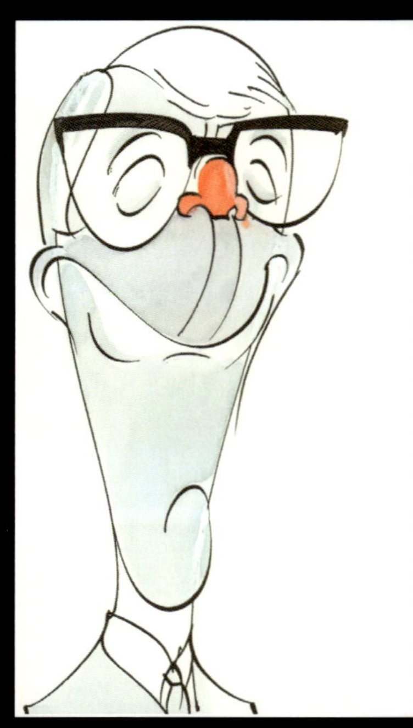

JOHN MAJOR

PRIME MINISTER 1990–1997

Oh yes! Indeed! A most unmemorable, if not insignificant, fellow. Grey was his colour, grey were his days . . . and ours too. Said to be one of the worst prime ministers ever, and that's going some. Think Neville Chamberlain.

I feel I never really got him. Maybe it was lack of interest on my part. The later drawings were better than the first attempts.

I met him once: nice man; fond of a hot Currie, the dark horse.

Black Wednesday (16 September 1992) was the day when Britain crashed out of the European Exchange Rate Mechanism, despite the raising of interest rates to 15 per cent and the spending of billions in a frantic attempt to keep the pound within the range allowed. It was a blow from which the Major government never recovered. Chancellor Norman Lamont survived long enough for a bare bones budget in the new year (top left), and subsequently to announce that the country was learning how to walk again after a recession and the ERM disaster (bottom right), but in May 1993 he was shoved onto his sword.

(TOP) June 1995, and Major's standing among his Cabinet colleagues was at an all-time low. In a put-up-or-shut-up move, he resigned the leadership and stood for re-election. Some thought he wouldn't survive the move. It paid off, but his fortunes didn't improve.

(RIGHT/BELOW) Major, the circus performer's son, as a magician at the Blackpool conference in October 1995, where he was expected to produce some startling new ideas. He didn't.

HOW DO YOU LIKE YOUR BEEF DONE?

BURNT PLEASE

(OPPOSITE) Major's growing woes in 1996, set in the context of the continuing problem of mad cow disease. Foreign Secretary Malcolm Rifkind attempts to administer a revitalising shot (bottom right).

(RIGHT) The long-standing feud within Tory ranks over European policy continued right up to (and beyond) the 1997 election. The Tory manifesto kept options open on joining the single currency, but said a firm no to a federal Europe. Chancellor Ken Clarke was a leading pro-European in the Cabinet.

(BELOW LEFT) May 1996, and the French have refused to import British beef. Major, seated on a mad cow, fires a salvo across the Channel.

(BELOW RIGHT) Rifkind, Clarke and Major as the three wise monkeys in February 1997.

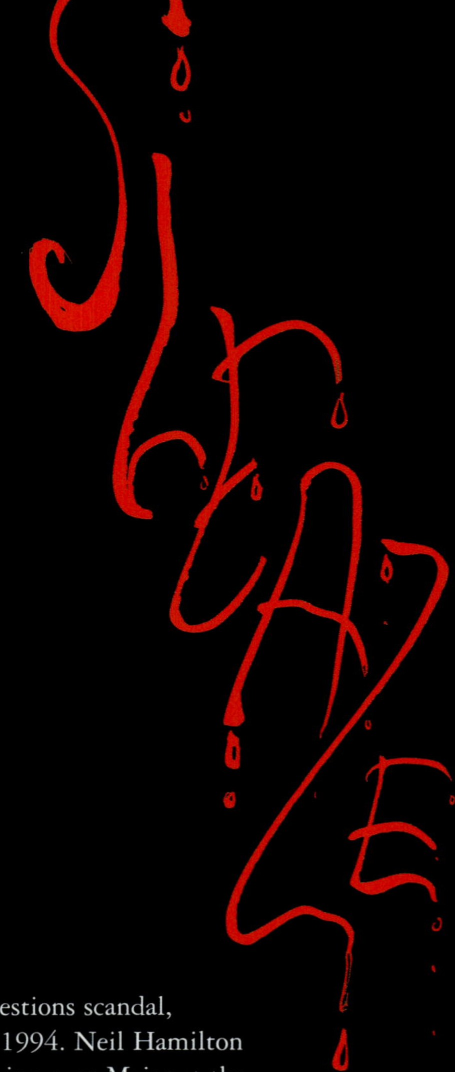

The cash-for-questions scandal, which broke in 1994. Neil Hamilton (the wave smashing over Major at the party conference in Bournemouth) was among those accused of trousering money in brown envelopes in exchange for parliamentary questions.

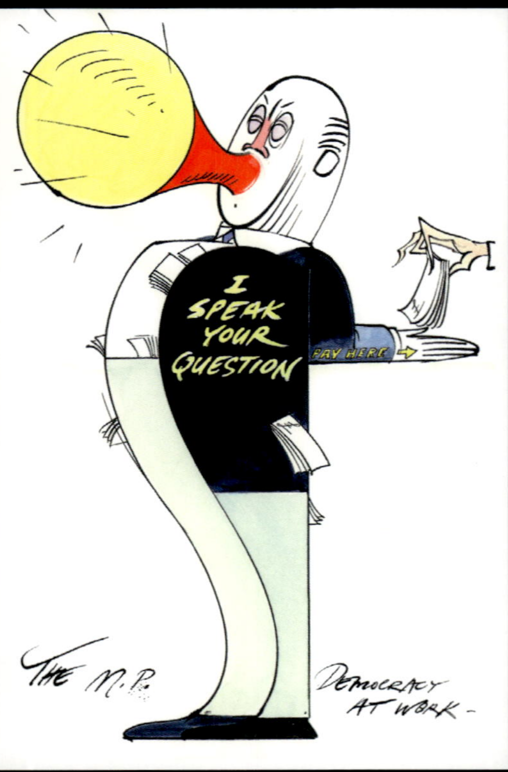

HEAVY SLEAZE AT BOURNEMOUTH

TODAY'S' MAN

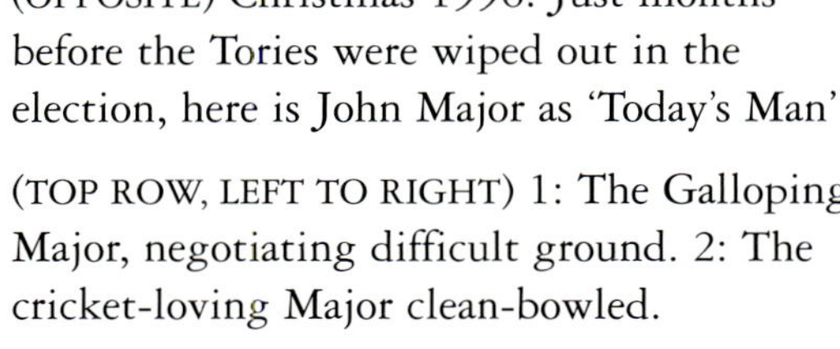

(OPPOSITE) Christmas 1996. Just months before the Tories were wiped out in the election, here is John Major as 'Today's Man'.

(TOP ROW, LEFT TO RIGHT) 1: The Galloping Major, negotiating difficult ground. 2: The cricket-loving Major clean-bowled. 3: Stabbed in the back and dead as a dodo in June 1993, just after Lamont got the heave-ho.

(BOTTOM ROW FROM LEFT TO RIGHT) 1: U-turn if you want to – I'm for turning too. In the 1994 European elections, the Tories took a pasting: their MEPs almost halved in number to just eighteen. 2: By 1995 there was a better chance of spotting Nessie than a Tory politician in Scotland. 3: Not waving, but drowning.

MAJOR **ENJOYS A HOT CURRIE**

(LEFT) As Junior Minister of Health, Edwina Currie promoted the use of condoms in the fight against Aids, advice I assume she heeded while immersed in an affair with . . .

(BELOW) John Major, who is trying to cover his shame with a copy of Currie's diaries, in which she disclosed that the former PM had been her lover between 1984 and 1988. Major had, of course, in an effort to stem a Tory tide of salacious sleaze, embarked on something of a crusade under a 'Back to Basics' banner. Whoops.

(OPPOSITE) An example of the terrible situations we cartoonists are sometimes forced to depict.

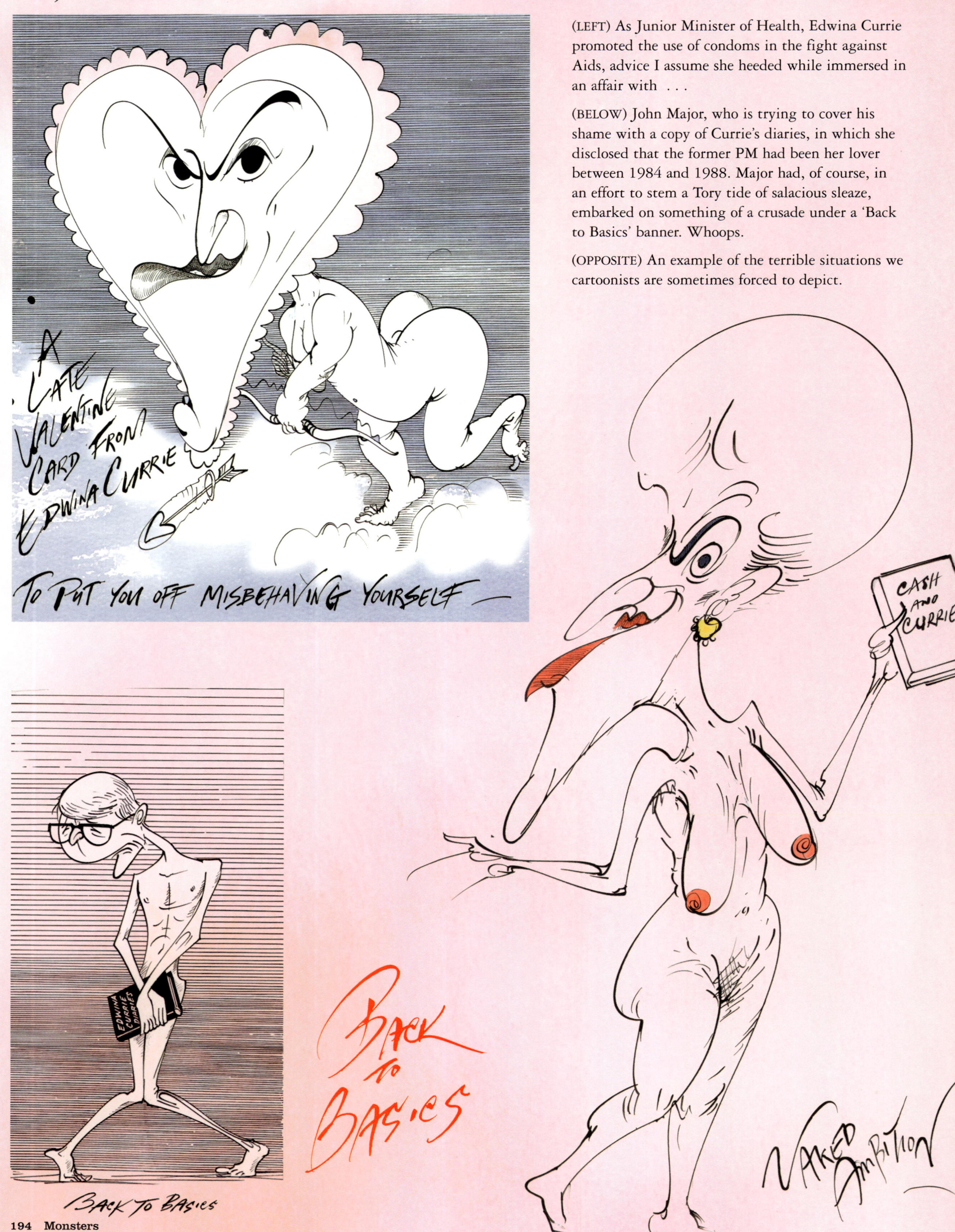

A GHASTLY THOUGHT.

OH YES!

MORE SLEAZE
EVEN MORE SLEAZE
MORE SLEAZE
COMPROMISING PICTURE (EXCLUSIVE)
WIRRAL 7,888 MAJORITY
7,887
7,886
JOHN MAJOR'S CLONING NIGHTMARE
JOHN MAJOR PREPARES TO LEAVE No. 10 DOWNING STREET WITH DIGNITY.

OPPOSITE

(TOP LEFT) In the run-up to the 1997 election, those sleazy stories and allegations kept on coming.

(BELOW LEFT) During the day, Major mounted his soapbox; at night he was forced to count Blair-majority sheep to get to sleep.

(BELOW RIGHT) Preparing for the end.

THIS PAGE

(ABOVE) After years of Tory recalcitrance the German Chancellor Helmut Kohl relishes the opportunity to deal with a more Euro-friendly Brit.

(LEFT) As the end approaches the PM stag is torn apart by backbench hounds.

TORY LEADERS

(TOP LEFT) The Tories rummage around for a new leader in May 1997.

(ABOVE) Once Hague was dumped after the 2001 election, it was Iain Duncan Smith's turn. The Tories seemed unable to make a good decision: IDS was weak and ineffective and was very soon dispatched and thrown into the Tory waste bin with Hague, Major and Thatcher (OPPOSITE TOP RIGHT)

(LEFT) William Hague is threatened by Michael Portillo during the fight for the leadership.

(ABOVE) In 2003, Michael Howard rose from the ranks as the new Tory leader. Ann Widdecombe had once memorably said 'he had something of the night about him' (she should know). This gave me a great opportunity to draw him as a Dracula-like bloodsucking vampire.

(RIGHT) David Cameron and David Davis in a fight for the leadership of the Tory party in 2005. During a joint interview on BBC Radio's *Woman's Hour* they were asked what kind of underwear they favoured, jockey briefs or boxer shorts.

LIBERAL DEMOCRATS

(RIGHT) Contenders for the Lib Dem leadership in 2006: a chronologically challenged Menzies Campbell, Chris Huhne and Simon Hughes (holding on for dear life). The falling figure is Home Affairs spokesman Mark Oaten, who pulled out of the race early after revelations of an affair with a male prostitute.

(LEFT) Jeremy Thorpe, who resigned the leadership of the Liberal Party in 1976 amid much scandal.

(LEFT) Menzies Campbell, forever dogged by the age issue; Charles Kennedy, ousted for being a drunk; and (BELOW) David Steel, hoping for a coalition in 1976.

NEIL KINNOCK

(RIGHT) Neil Kinnock was leader of the Labour Party from 1983 to 1992. Skilful orator or waffler supreme – your choice.

(BELOW) Kinnock said it was his wife Glenys's shoes that caused him to fall on his arse and make a bloody fool of himself on the beach at a party conference in front of the assembled photographers. He was trying to stop them getting wet. So you see, it was his gallantry that brought him down. Some hope. The disastrous Sheffield rally in 1992 was a good candidate for that: like an American president in a glamorous promotional film by Hugh Hudson, Kinnock shouted, 'Well all right! Well all right!' while punching the air with all the assuredness of someone who knew he was going to win. He then proceeded to lose.

‘Big things are expected of us, and nothing big ever came of being small’

Fun in the Oval Orifice! Disbarred, perjured, impeached adulterer. That was Bill Clinton. But for all that he’s regarded as a charming, good old boy.

BILL CLINTON

US PRESIDENT 1993–2001

I DID NOT
HAVE SEX WITH THAT WOMEN!

(OPPOSITE) In January 1998, with a defiant Hillary by his side, Clinton denied having 'sexual relations' with White House intern Monica Lewinsky. For her part, Ms Lewinsky testified that she and the President had had ten sexual encounters, and on nine of those occasions she performed oral sex.

(BELOW) Tales surfaced of sexual harassment and improper advances stretching back to Clinton's days as Governor of Arkansas.

(RIGHT) The ambitious Hillary Clinton works her man with a painted smile.

(ABOVE FROM LEFT TO RIGHT) June 1995, and Clinton contemplates whether or not to become enmeshed in the troubles in Bosnia.

In September 1994, Clinton sent an armada to Haiti to reinstate President Jean-Bertrand Aristide – who had been ousted in a bloody coup in 1991 by General Raoul Cedras – and restore democracy in that country. A dubious democracy, though.

Much to John Major's annoyance, in March 1995 Clinton unrolled the red carpet in New York for Sinn Fein's Gerry Adams, to help with the Irish American vote. Many Irish Americans subscribed to the IRA.

(RIGHT) Clinton as Paul Bunyan, the lumberjack hero of American folklore, the big man who feared nothing.

(BOTTOM RIGHT) There was talk of Clinton's impeachment in December 1998, Zippergate and the Whitewater land deal scandal from his Arkansas days having heavily dented his presidency. Would Clinton be emasculated *à la* John Wayne Bobbitt, whose wife famously lopped off a portion of his member and threw it out of a car window?

TONY BLAIR

PRIME MINISTER 1997–2007

I was disappointed and angry with Blair. He seemed to begin so promisingly, if a little flashily; in contrast to Major's greyness and hopelessness he did seem a good thing.

But then he fell in with the ghastly George Bush and turned into a glib, slippery liar. He lied to us all about being forty-five minutes away from destruction by Saddam.

I met Blair once at a dinner party. Someone around the table remarked that my drawings were savage. 'Oh!' said Blair. 'I don't think they're all that savage.' Right, I thought. Must try harder.

He was with us for ten years. It felt like an age, and his image was printed on our everyday lives, but, almost magically, when he left office he was forgotten within a few weeks. Here today, gone tomorrow. His ears grew bigger and bigger over that time . . .

‘The truth is, you can’t go on for ever’

A giddy Tony Blair on the upturned finger of his Director of Communications and Strategy, Alastair Campbell (the finger next to it was often upturned in the direction of the press).

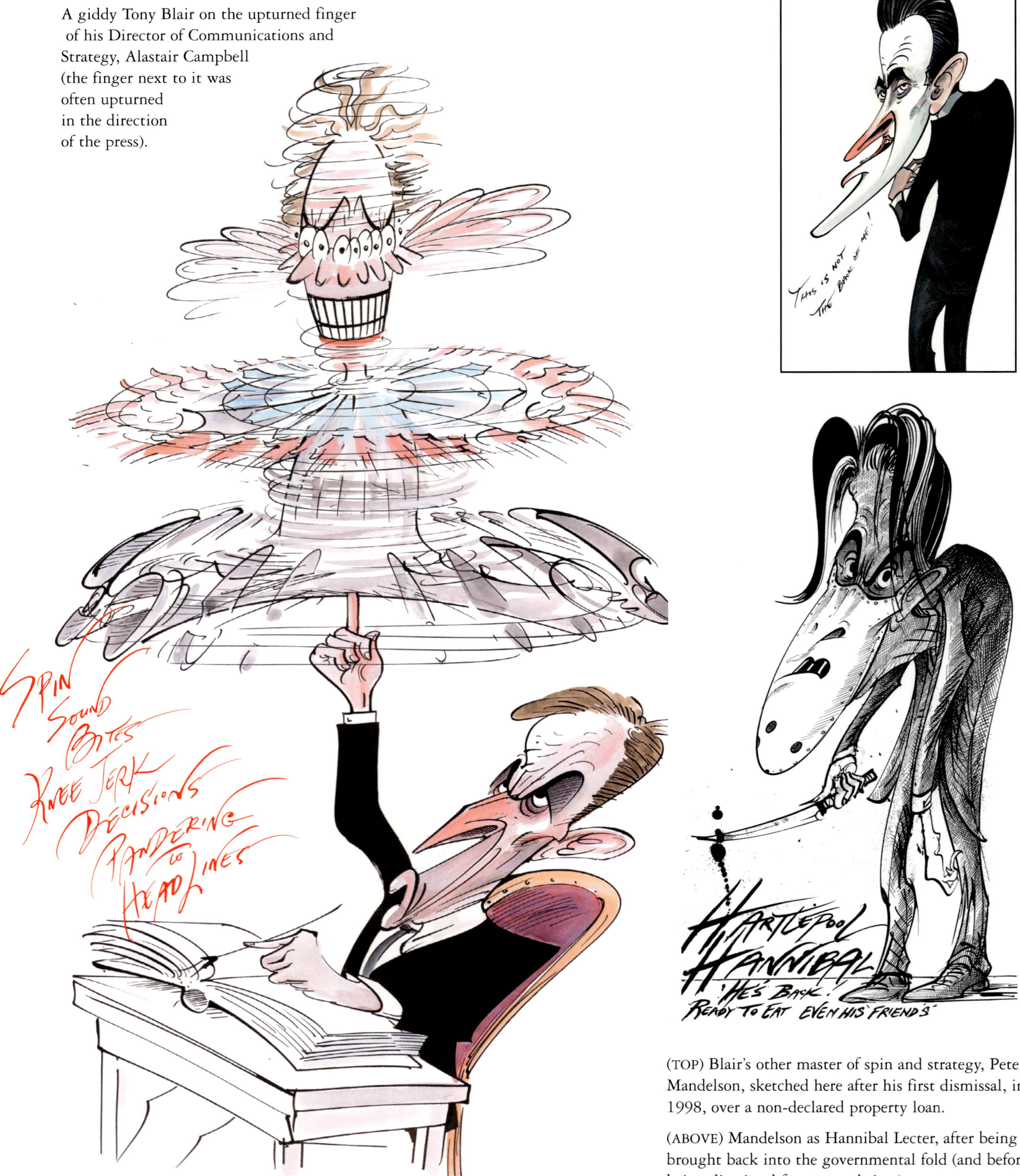

(TOP) Blair's other master of spin and strategy, Peter Mandelson, sketched here after his first dismissal, in 1998, over a non-declared property loan.

(ABOVE) Mandelson as Hannibal Lecter, after being brought back into the governmental fold (and before being dismissed for a second time).

(TOP LEFT) During elections, Blair and Brown were forced to put on a pretence of unity.

(ABOVE) Blair refusing to relinquish the prime ministerial crown – a popular Westminster soap opera that ran for years.

(LEFT) Blair as the hunchbacked Richard III, holding on to power to the last.

In May 2004 there was a rumpus in the House of Commons when Fathers for Justice activists threw a condom full of purple powder at Blair during PMQs. Brown, getting on as badly as ever with the PM, re-enacts the episode.

August 2005, and Home Secretary Charles Clarke (Big Ears) and Tony Blair (Noddy with big ears) roll with plans to detain terror suspects without charge.

Deputy Leader of the Labour Party John Prescott made several gaffes while in office; here I recall the affair with his diary secretary Tracey Temple (his trousers are round his ankles), calling George Bush a 'crap cowboy', and being photographed playing croquet at his grace-and-favour home Dorneywood when he was supposed to be running the country in Blair's absence.

(RIGHT) Foreign Secretary Margaret Beckett gazes into her crystal ball as she sits outside her caravan (she and her husband are enthusiastic caravanners).

Double nanny trouble. (BELOW) In November 2004, Home Secretary David Blunkett was accused of nannying the country by bringing in too many rules and restrictions; and (RIGHT) just a few weeks later, Nanny Blunkett was accused of obtaining a visa for the au pair of his ex-lover.

(RIGHT) Blunkett's affair with Kimberly Quinn, the American publisher of the *Spectator*, which led to his resignation.

Blair opposed Ken Livingstone's candidacy for Mayor of London, so Red Ken left the Labour Party, saddled up as an independent and took to the streets. In 2000, he succeeded in robbing Blair and his official choice Frank Dobson of the post.

THEN TONY MET A FRIEND
DESK OF THE PRESIDENT
TONY

A series of drawings showing how a loving bond quickly developed between Blair and his new pal George Bush.

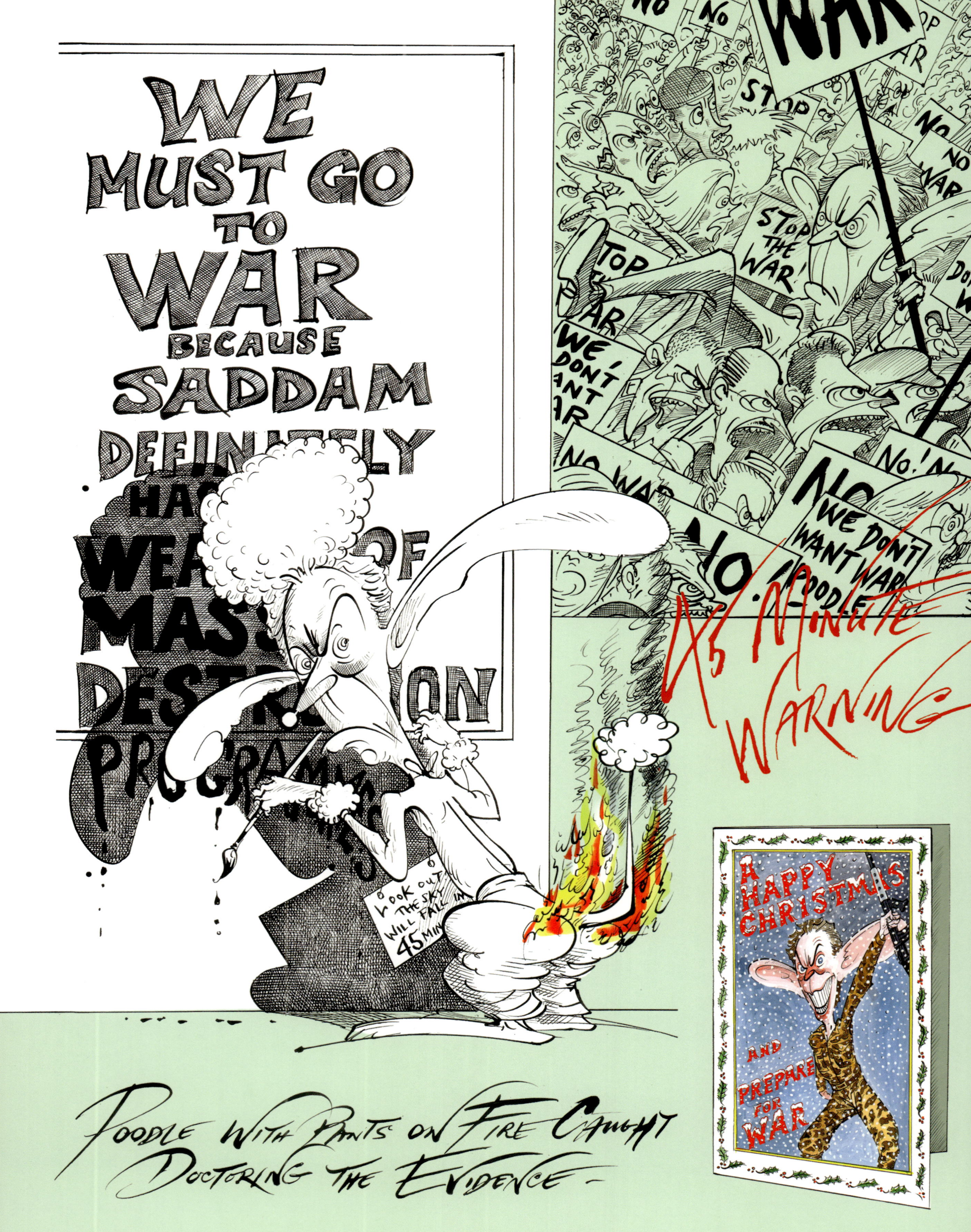

Poodle With Pants on Fire Caught Doctoring the Evidence

(OPPOSITE: (FAR LEFT) July, and Tony 'Poodle' Blair is in a spot of bother, accused of 'sexing up' the case for war against Iraq. Even if Saddam didn't have weapons of mass destruction, he had a WMD *programme* . . . (TOP RIGHT) In March 2003, as coalition forces opened their campaign, thousands of Stop the War protesters took to the streets throughout Britain and other parts of the world. (RIGHT) Blair's card for Christmas 2002. He was determined to support his pal George Bush and take us all into the war with Iraq.

THIS PAGE: (ABOVE) In October 2004, Blair was asked in the House of Commons to apologise for the war, by which time he was heartily sick of people banging on about the subject. (RIGHT) Poodle Blair reads the Joint Intelligence Committee report, which actually stated that intelligence on Saddam and WMD was 'limited' and based mainly on 'assessment'.

ONWARD
THE BEARERS

(OPPOSITE)
Bush and Blair persist in their belief that the war in Iraq is worth the fight. The military of both nations bear the full weight of this.

(LEFT) When Corporal Gordon Pritchard was killed early in 2006 – the 100th British soldier to die in Iraq – Blair felt obliged to make sense of the fiasco.

No longer the poodle, now the marionette: Bush operating Blair, who in turn twitches the threads of his Foreign Secretary Margaret Beckett.

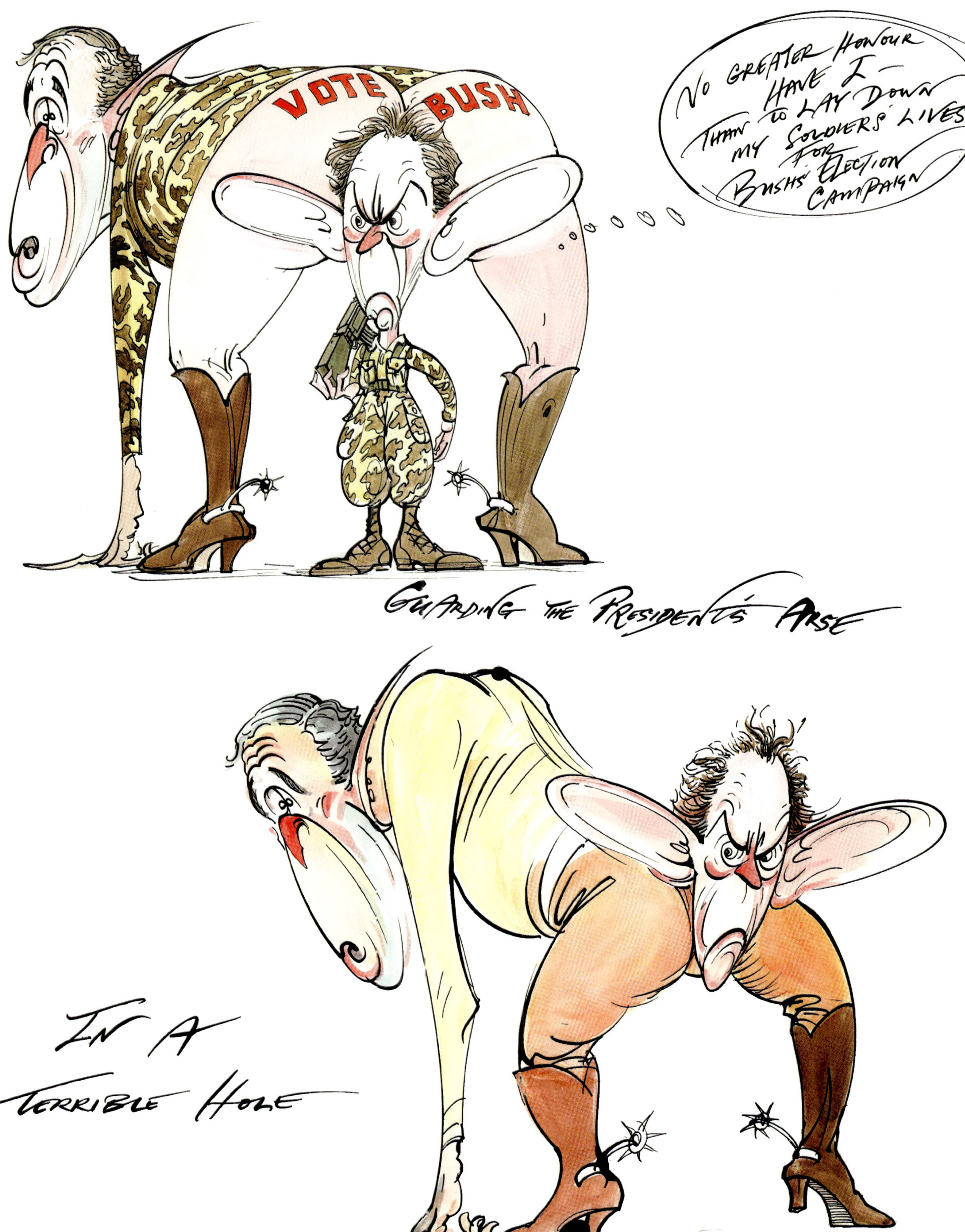
VOTE
BUSH
NO GREATER HONOUR HAVE I THAN TO LAY DOWN MY SOLDIERS' LIVES FOR BUSH'S ELECTION CAMPAIGN
GUARDING THE PRESIDENT'S ARSE
IN A TERRIBLE HOLE

The Grim Reaper forces a cammed-up Blair and Bush to contemplate their track record (December 2006).

In an interview with Michael Parkinson in March 2006, the devoutly Christian Blair announced that he believed God would judge him over his decision to go to war with Iraq.

(BELOW) In December 2007, after leaving office, Blair was received into the Catholic Church.

BLOATED

STUFFED
TERRORIST PUDDING
IRAQI STUFFING
BUSH TURKEY
BURP!
HUNT WINE
BLUNKETT PIE
GORDON BROWN SAUCE

(OPPOSITE) An overly rich and complex meal leaves Blair feeling uncomfortable.

(THIS PAGE) Blair needs several buckets in his attempt to digest the unwholesome findings of both the Butler inquiry into the intelligence the British government had about Iraq and WMDs, and the Hutton inquiry into the death of Dr David Kelly, but neither of them lay any blame at the PM's door. There were mutterings in the Commons that key questions that needed answers had not been addressed.

Blair denied accusations of offering peerages for cash after four people he nominated for honours were found to have made highly generous contributions to the party coffers without the knowledge of Labour's treasurer or other elected officials. Like James Bond in *Goldfinger*, he was in a bind, the crown jewels exposed.

(ABOVE) Blair the ingénu discovers for the first time chief fundraiser Lord Levy busy at work and applies some Rumsfeldian logic to the situation.

(TOP RIGHT) He bears gifts.

(RIGHT) He sells gifts.

(BELOW) Blair binge-drinking in January 2005.

(RIGHT) Twenty-four-hour drinking was introduced in November 2005. The landlord of the Leaky Ship pulls a pint while Gordon Brown tries to call time – on the whole shebang.

(OPPOSITE) A sketch from February 2007 depicting the ruination of Blair's administration, mired as it was in the cash for honours investigation, the ghastly aftermath of the Iraq war, and tawdry issues such as super casinos and binge-drinking on Britain's streets.

RUINED
JUST WANT TO GET ON WITH THE JOB
GAMBLING HAS MADE ME WHAT I AM!
TIME TO BUGGER OFF
SPIN
LEVY
CASH FOR HONOURS
FIRST P.M. INVOLVED CRIMINAL INQUIRY

A series of drawings from the summer of 2006, when Blair became the first serving prime minister to be questioned by police as part of a criminal investigation (cash for honours). As he contemplates his end, should he do the right thing? Yes, he should.

LINE DO NOT CROSS CRIME SCENE POLICE LINE DO NOT CROSS CRIME SCEN
CASH FOR HONOURS POLICE REPORT TO CROWN PROSECUTION
SERIOUS WRONG DOINGS
RUTH TURNER
BLAIR QUESTIONED BY POLICE

June 2007, and the fateful and long-awaited day for the handover of power to Gordon Brown – first promised, allegedly, in 1994 over a meal in Islington's Granita restaurant – finally arrived. The shifty bugger was yanked off stage, closed down and thrown out of Number Ten.

UNDER NEW
MANAGEMENT
NO SCANDALS NO SPIN
ON YOUR WAY
YOU SHIFTY BUGGER
HONEST
GORDON
(NOTHING TO
DO WITH THE
PREVIOUS
MOB.)
REMOVAL DAY

Snapshots of Blair's legacy as his days at Number Ten drew to a close.

90 DAYS DETENTION WITHOUT TRIAL
MY STORY
TONY BLAIR
I WAS CAPTURED BY GEORGE BUSH AND MADE TO DO THE MOST HIDEOUS THINGS
BLOOD
Blair's Memoires

Still with an eye on that legacy (or conscience), despite the blood on his hands. During his final PMQs in June 2007, Blair announced that his 'absolute priority' would be to bring about a two-state solution to the Israel–Palestine conflict. One Palestinian daily very generously called Blair's appointment as peace envoy 'a strange choice'.

Middle East Peace Envoy

IS IT A BIRD?
IS IT A PLANE?
NO! IT'S A
FUCKING DISASTER

Wonderful, terrific, fantastic, laugh-a-minute. I couldn't want for more – an absolute dream to draw. But as American president he is the dangerous moron who put all our lives in peril. A disastrously confused, simple monster. He thinks he's funny and he certainly is a walking joke. A horrible, sick, fatal joke – I draw him as a bewildered ape, his close-set eyes beneath a wrinkled and puzzled brow, his knuckles scraping the ground as he wanders aimlessly, crushing all beneath him, his arse stuck out behind with Iraq branded on his hide. All in the name of God.

'Bring them on . . . '

GEORGE W. BUSH

PRESIDENT 2001 . . .

The year 2000, and George Bush, son of George Bush, having squeezed past Al Gore, is elected the 43rd President of the United States.

'Dubya' was formerly the Governor of Texas, a state that still believes in the death penalty. A promising background for the most powerful man in the world . . .

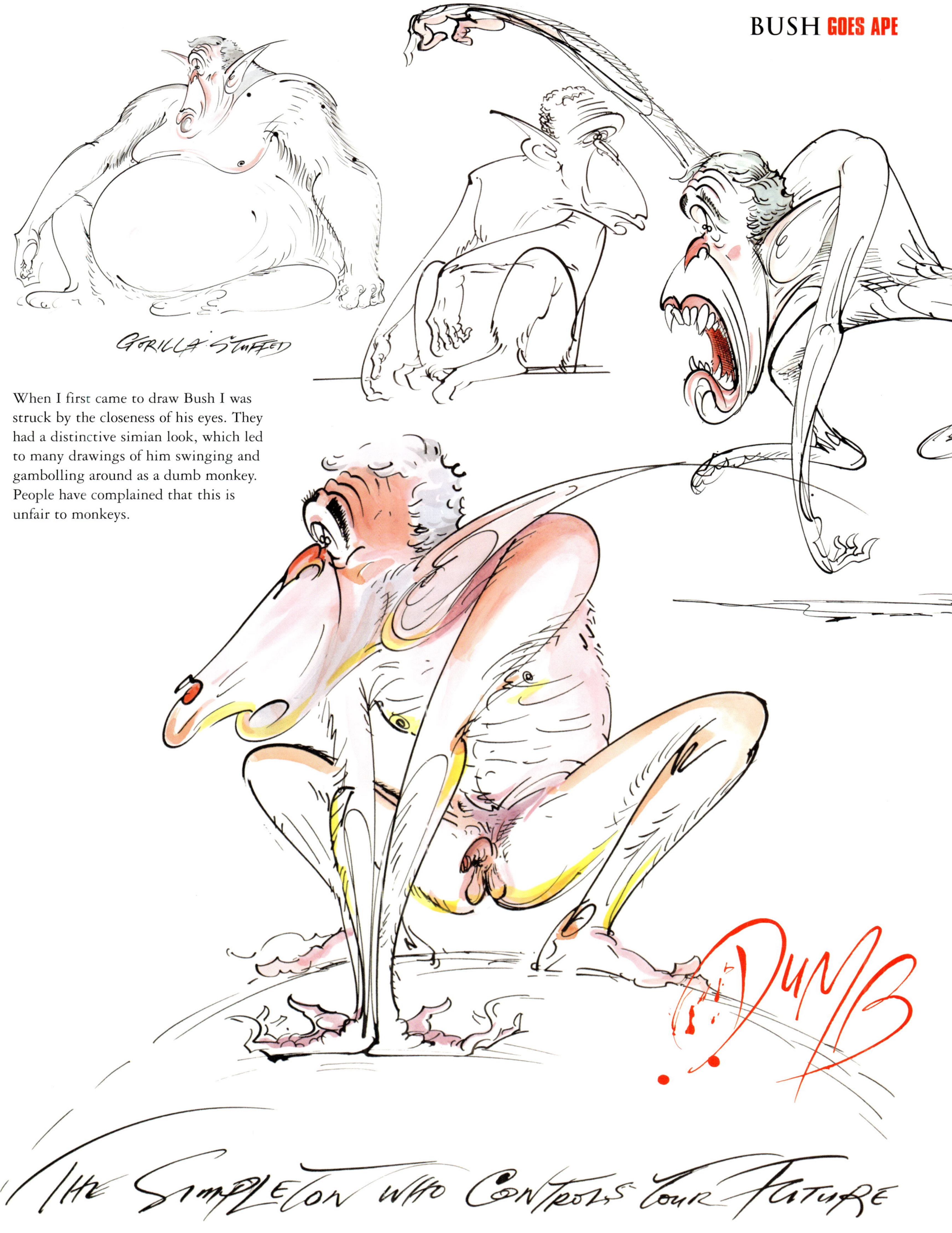

When I first came to draw Bush I was struck by the closeness of his eyes. They had a distinctive simian look, which led to many drawings of him swinging and gambolling around as a dumb monkey. People have complained that this is unfair to monkeys.

The Twin Towers burn on 11 September 2001.

(ABOVE) Bush was told the bad news while he was reading to a class of young children. At first he seemed unable to comprehend what had happened, and continued reading.

(BELOW) Almost from the moment the planes hit, Bush moved on to a war footing, vowing to root out the al-Qaeda network and all those who aided or harboured them, whatever the cost.

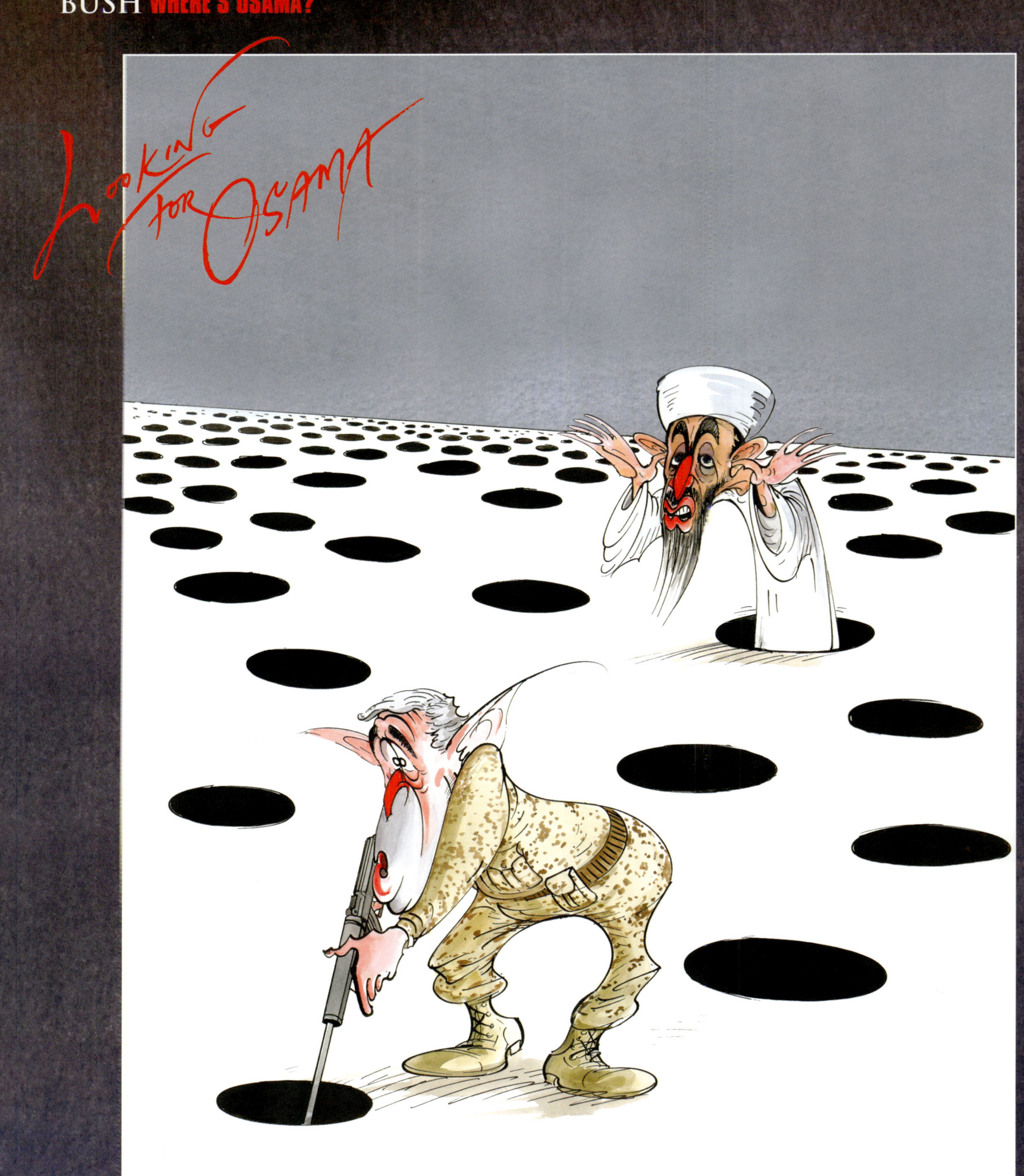

Bush promised to smoke out Osama bin Laden, heavily implicated in the 9/11 plot, who was said to be hiding in the warren-like mountains of Afghanistan.

The Boogie Man. As in Britain, the preparation of the public for war was underpinned by one cherished strategy above all: scare the living bejesus out of them and they'll go along with it. (Just a spoonful of panic helps the populace stay down . . .)

Bush tries to swat Saddam Hussein. Once upon a time they sold him weapons; now he's just a pesky varmint.

OPPOSITE

(FAR LEFT) Once it was clear that Iraq was in breach of UN resolution 1441, which required Saddam to disarm voluntarily, in the early months of 2003 Blair was instrumental in persuading Bush to seek a second resolution authorising war. None was forthcoming. On 20 March, in a live television address, Bush confirmed that the campaign to topple Saddam had begun with air strikes on Baghdad. UN Secretary-General Kofi Annan said his thoughts were with the ordinary people of Iraq.

(FAR RIGHT) By April, Iraq had exploded into chaos.

WAR
FRIENDLY FIRE
CHAOS
WHY ARE THEY SO IRRESPONSIBLE?
LIBERTY

(LEFT) Bush Man starts bush fire.

(OPPOSITE) Belligerent Secretary of Defense Donald Rumsfeld, Dick Cheney and Condoleezza Rice encourage all to make war on Iraq.

COME ON IN THE WAR'S LOVEL

PSSSST! SORRY ABOUT THAT
C.I.A.
JUST FOLLOWING TRADITION
IRAQ U.S. DEAD
VOTE BUSH 2004
GET U.S. OUT
PULL OUT
BRING OUR TROOPS HOME
MISTAKE
AMERICAN DEATH TOLL

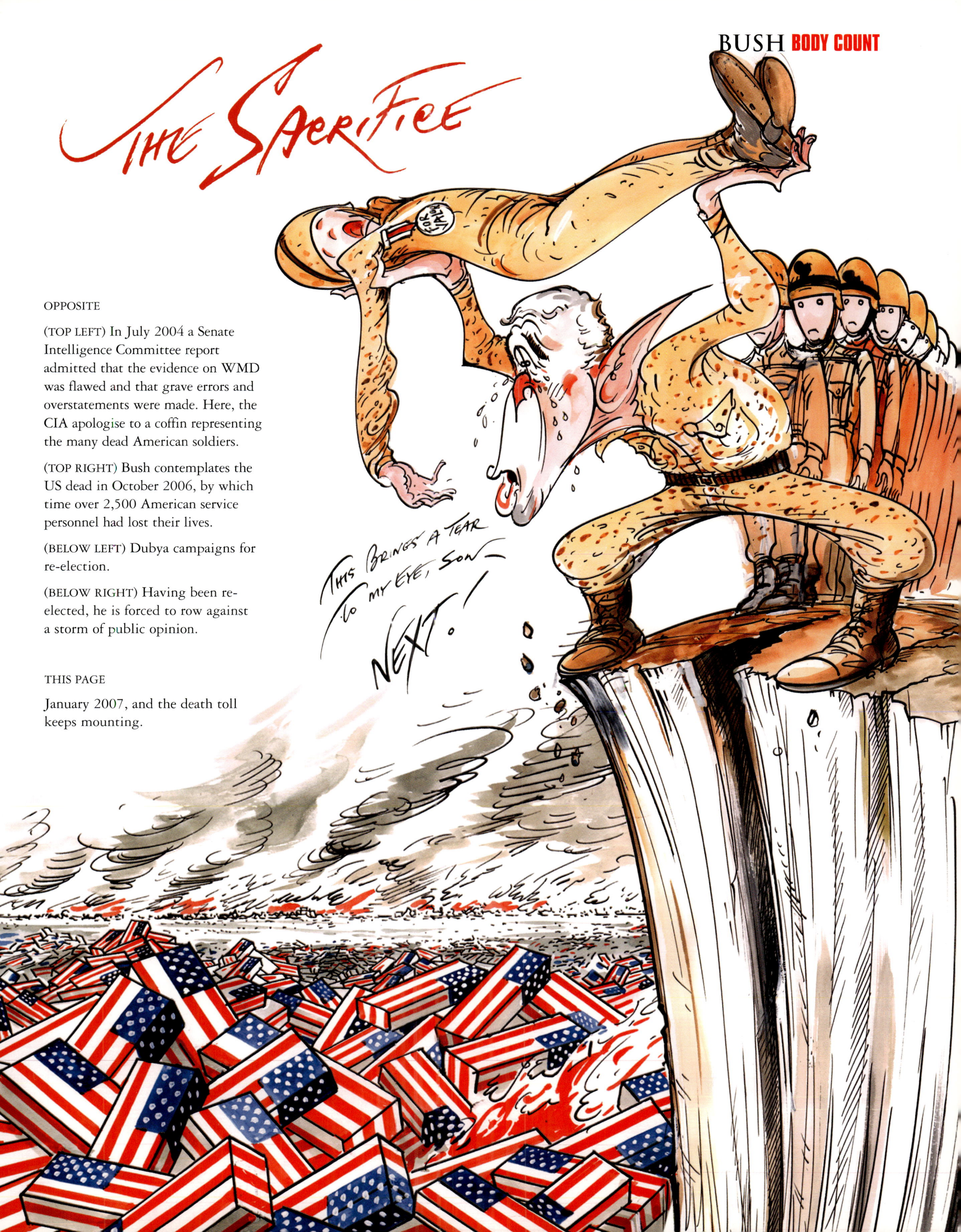

OPPOSITE

(TOP LEFT) In July 2004 a Senate Intelligence Committee report admitted that the evidence on WMD was flawed and that grave errors and overstatements were made. Here, the CIA apologise to a coffin representing the many dead American soldiers.

(TOP RIGHT) Bush contemplates the US dead in October 2006, by which time over 2,500 American service personnel had lost their lives.

(BELOW LEFT) Dubya campaigns for re-election.

(BELOW RIGHT) Having been re-elected, he is forced to row against a storm of public opinion.

THIS PAGE

January 2007, and the death toll keeps mounting.

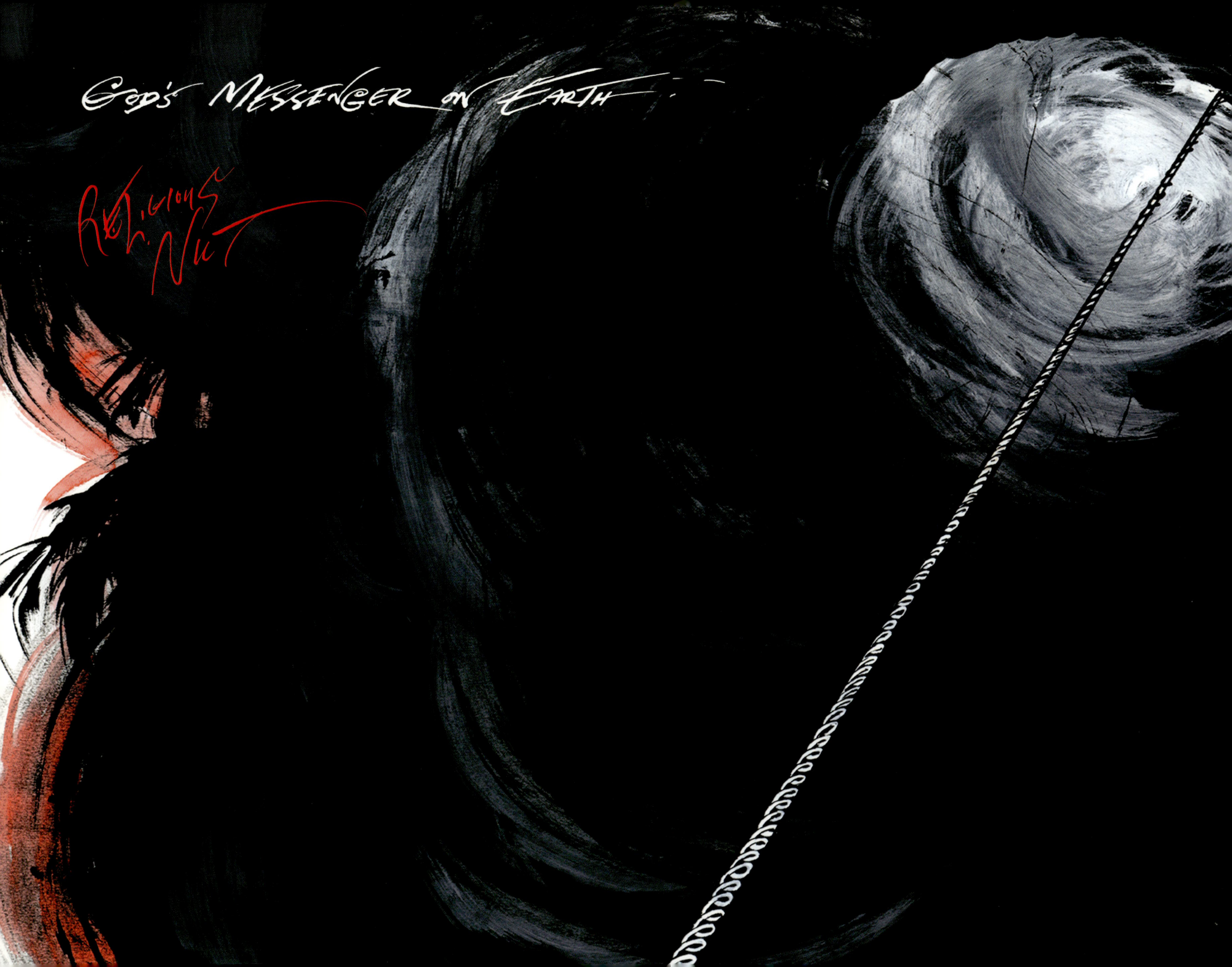
GOD'S MESSENGER ON EARTH
RELIGIOUS NUT

Bush, the ardent Christian, on the blower in October 2005.

TORTURE
ALL IN THE NAME OF GOD

(OPPOSITE) In 2004 photos began to emerge of prisoner abuse at the American facility Abu Ghraib in Iraq. Bush perches on the bodies of tortured internees, arranged in an identical way to one of the released images.

(RIGHT) One of the victims appears on Bush's desk in the Oval Office. The Poodle gulps as he knows this is a serious blow to the coalition's moral standing.

More reflection on the coalition's conduct of the War on Terror. In December 2005, Blair defended the secret transfer of terrorist suspects, or 'extraordinary rendition', and denied that individuals were being moved to any country or destination that used torture. Bush's Secretary of State Condoleezza Rice echoed those words.

I drew Bush as the giant ape, inspired by the remake of the movie *King Kong*.

In May 2004, Donald Rumsfeld publicly apologised for the torturing of detainees at Abu Ghraib. It struck me as mealy-mouthed and two-faced. Just a few months later, three British men held for over two years at Guantanamo Bay returned to Britain alleging abuse and humiliation at the hands of their American hosts.

(INSET) Mid-term elections in October 2006.

(RIGHT) As the 2004 election approaches, Bush is worried that the piles of dead American bodies in Iraq will scupper his chances of a second term.

What did they do? Astonishingly, in November 2004 Bush was given another four years in charge by the American electorate.

Shock and Awe

(ABOVE) Less than a year after re-election, Dubya went looking for more trouble.

(RIGHT) In a homage to the scene from Stanley Kubrick's *Dr Strangelove*, Bush plummets towards Iran on the back of a missile.

(ABOVE) Bush and Blair try to get some sleep.

(MAIN PICTURE) August 2007. The Grim Reaper calls on Bush to survey his ghastly work.

'YO BUSH
OL' BUDDY
HOW WE DOIN'?

Bambi, Dumbo and two lame ducks.

In his live broadcast in March 2003, Bush had warned that the campaign to 'disarm Iraq and free its people' could be 'longer and more difficult than some predict'. Just a few years later these words had morphed from a caution into an understatement. My Kiplingesque take on this: the toothy, bloody jaws of the Iraq crocodile pulling the Republican elephant down into the mire.

JEEZ! DID I DO ALL THAT?

Dubya is dumbfounded by the mess he has created.

A skeletal Blair dragging his ball and chain ekes out his time in office to the ten-year mark. At last, in June 2007, he stood down, leaving the way open for a heavyweight bruiser.

GORDON BROWN

PRIME MINISTER 2007 . . .

'Let the work of change begin . . .'

The clunking fist, Blair called him. And clunking is what he is. No excitement, no joy, dull, dour and very unexciting to draw. Brown looked forward for so long to achieving his heart's delight. But now he has it, he doesn't seem to enjoy it. Heavy of spirit, he has no ability to laugh at himself – in fact no ability to laugh at all. Even his smile is out of synch. I draw him as a clumsy, heavy figure in a dull black suit, rather fleshy with beetling brows and enormous ears.

When David Cameron became Tory leader in December 2005 he said it was time to end 'Punch and Judy' politics. But it was soon business as usual at the dispatch box, first with Blair, then with Brown. Cameron's blue-blooded heritage is said to grate on the classless Scot.

Ditherer!

In the autumn of 2007, Brown, newly installed as Prime Minister, couldn't decide whether to run for a quick election while things were good or hold off. His dithering lost him much of what sympathy and credibility he had.

Go on
Jump you wimp!
Go for it
Bottled out have we.
Go on scaredycat
Go on jump.
What's the matter with you?
Go on. Go on.

After the longest period of gestation known to political man, Brown rose, like a phoenix, from the rotting remains of B. Liar. But who was he? Nanny or puritan? Or both?

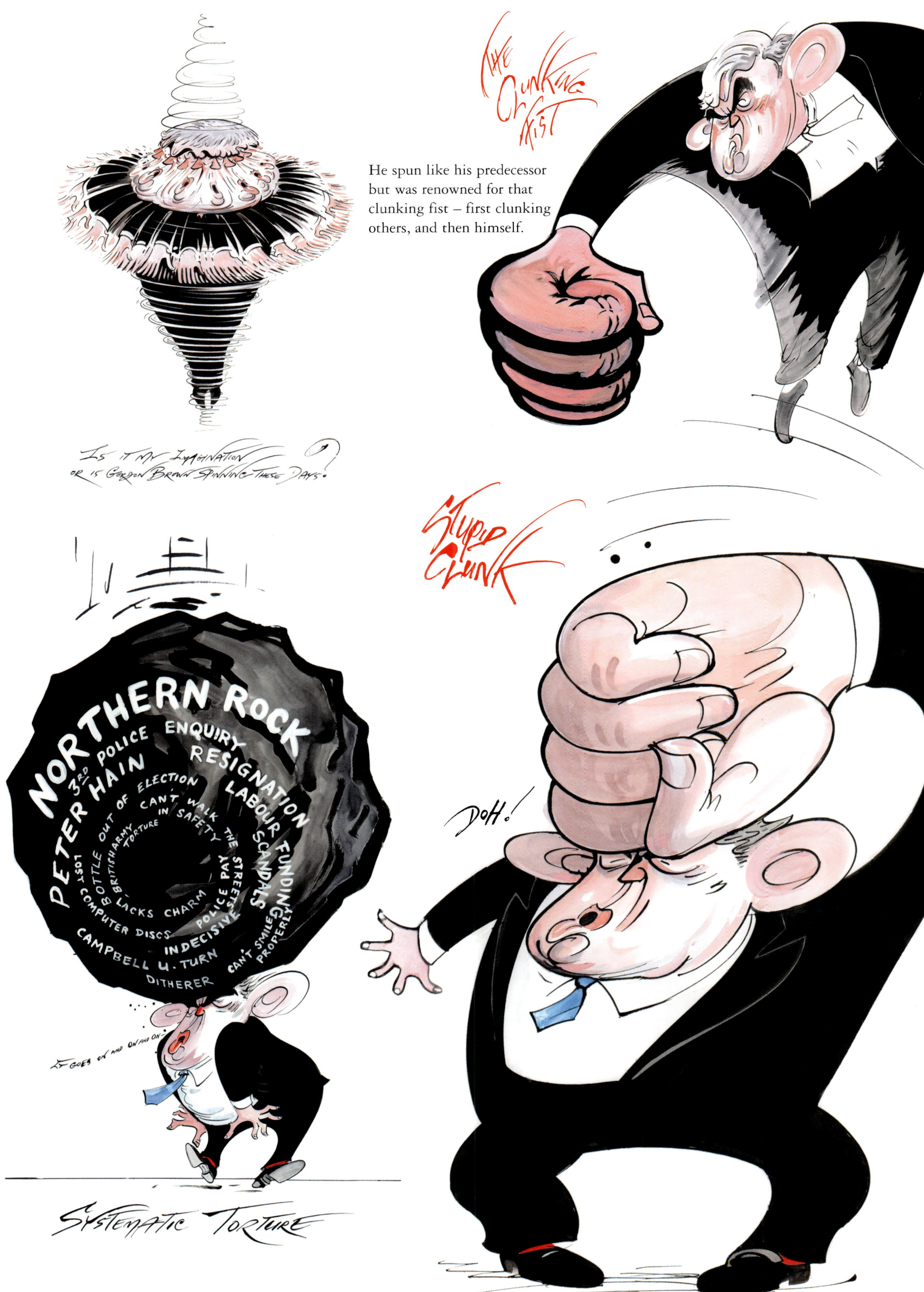

He spun like his predecessor but was renowned for that clunking fist – first clunking others, and then himself.

Bush tests the waters during Brown's visit to the US in the summer of 2007. Is Gordon going to be a poodle like his predecessor? A few teething problems, perhaps, but apparently so.

BROWN NOSING

THE NEW BOYS
OR ON AND ON AND ON

Smug Republican John McCain looks on as Democrats Hillary Clinton and Barack Obama fight it out; Hillary clings on by her fingernails. She is said to be running a dirty campaign and is accused of damaging the Democratic Party. Obama brings something new to politics. How will an African American or a woman fare against the all-American John McCain?

America, can you do it? We will probably see a Republican in the White House . . .

(ABOVE) Russian premier Vladimir Putin engineers the election of a puppet president to keep himself in power

(RIGHT) Foreign secretary David Milliband takes a meal with Vladimir Putin (a Russian diplomat had recently been poisoned at a sushi bar in Piccadilly, London).

AND ON AND ON . . .

(ABOVE) Some are crumbling while others step over the debris to have a crack at screwing up the world.

(RIGHT) Is David Milliband the heir to the crown?

Will Cameron be the next prime minister? Or, like all the others, will his political career end in failure?

AND ON . . .

AND ON . . .

AND ON

Mo

AND ON . . .

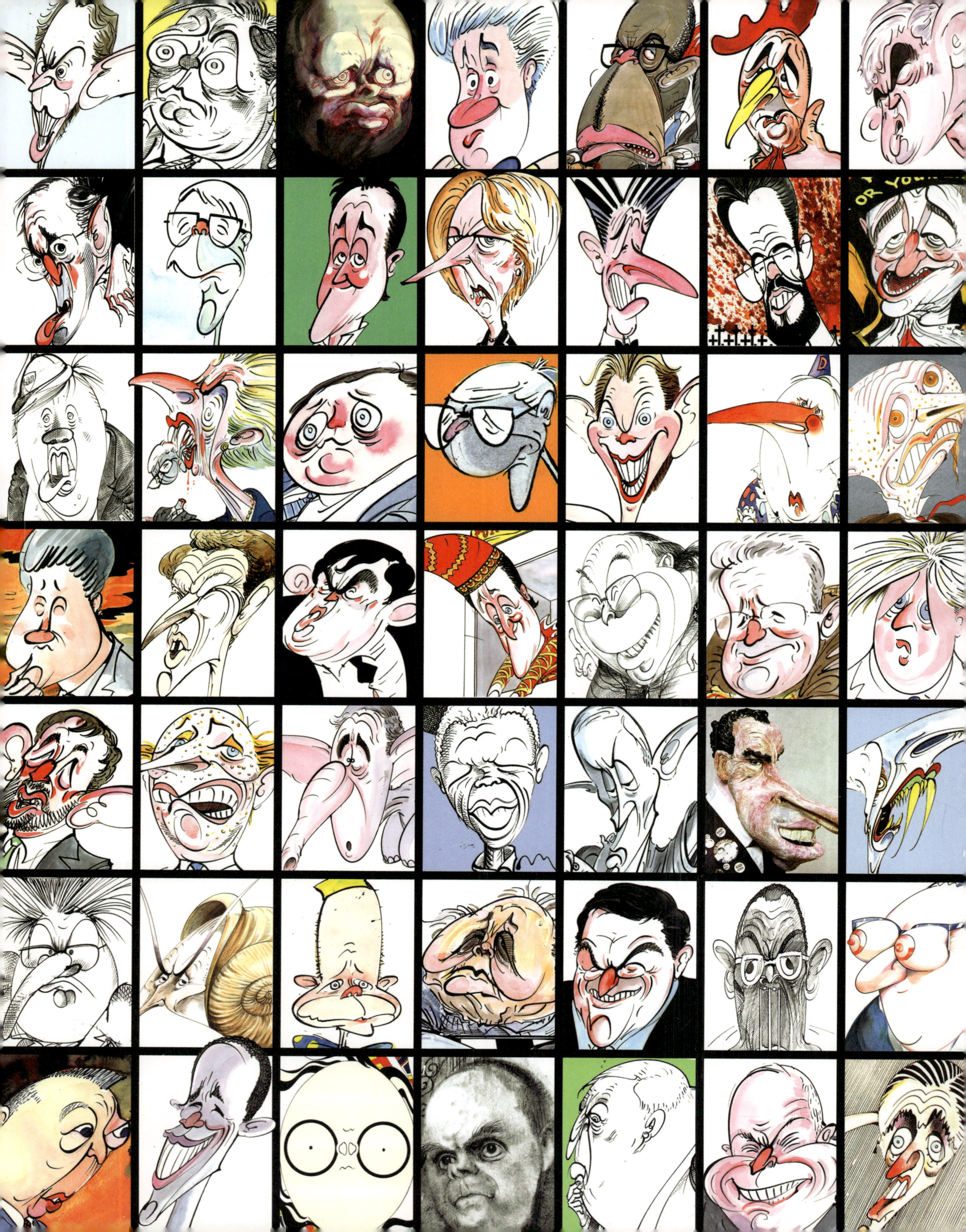